PASSPORT to CHINESE

100 MOST COMMONLY USED CHINESE CHARACTERS

Lin Snan

HEIAN

© 1995 Lin Shan

Published by
Heian International Inc.
1815 West 205th Street
Suite #301
Torrance, CA 90501
Web site: *www.heian.com*
E-mail address: *heianemail@heian.com*

Original edition published by SNP Publishing Pte Ltd, Singapore

Illustrations by Goh Ngoh Seng

First American Edition 1998
98 99 00 01 02 9 8 7 6 5 4 3 2 1

ISBN 0-89346-862-2

Printed in Singapore by Chong Moh Offset Printing Pte Ltd

FOREWORD

I wrote the foreword for Lin Shan's *Mandarin by Radio* when I was in the Ministry of Culture and was responsible for promoting the Speak Mandarin Campaign in March 1980. Changing people's speaking habit is a difficult task, especially in a multi-racial community. We have to take into account the feelings of the non-Chinese population and the resistance of the English-educated Chinese. However, after more than ten years, with the effort and support of those organizations and individuals who are concerned about the Chinese language and culture and the development of China's economy and the impact of the change in the domestic political climate, the Speak Mandarin Campaign has been very successful. The next step is to encourage more Chinese to learn Mandarin.

Some people think that the Chinese language is difficult to learn and there are too many characters. However, they overlook a characteristic of the Chinese language. It is more centralized. In other words, some characters are more frequently used. To read an ordinary article, we need to know more English words than Chinese characters. The 100 Chinese characters in this book can form 1,300 compound words and phrases and 100 idioms. Dialogues and passages on different themes can also be constructed with them.

As science and technology become more advanced, new terms will have to be created. An advantage of Chinese characters is that new terms can be created by combining characters. There is no need to create new characters. The average man will be able to read the Chinese newspaper if he knows about 1,000 common Chinese characters.

The 100 characters in this book are the most frequently used among 440,000 characters used in Chinese newspapers. They have been selected by computer for their frequent usage as they are the most viable characters. As a Chinese saying goes, the smartest housewife cannot cook a meal without rice. Lin Shan has very cleverly made full use of these 100 "rice" (characters) to make a lot of "delicious dishes". All these 100 Chinese characters can be used to form a lot of language patterns such as phrases, sentences, dialogues and even passages. For example, there are 20 descriptions of "he is a good man" and 95 ways of describing a person.

I sincerely hope that this book will stimulate more Chinese to learn Mandarin as it provides the environment for effective Chinese learning and enhances the promotion of the Chinese language and Chinese culture.

Dr Ow Chin Hock
Member of Parliament for Leng Kee Constituency

前 言

第一次为林珊的《华语广播课程》(Mandarin by Radio)写序是 1980 年 3 月。当时我在文化部任职，也负责推动"讲华语运动"。要改变人们语言习惯本来就是很困难的一件事。而且，在多元种族的环境下要顾及非华族的感受。再加上一些受英文教育华人的抗拒，所以"讲华语运动"在开始时，遇到许多困难和压力。但是，经过十多年来关心华族语言、文化的团体和个人锲而不舍的努力和支持，以及中国经济开放及国内政治气候改变的影响，"讲华语运动"目前已取得很大的成功。下一步的工作，应该是鼓励更多华人学习华文。

有些人认为华文难学，中文字繁多。但他们忽略了华文的一个特征，那就是汉字出现的频率很特殊，它比英文更集中，也就是说要看懂同样的普通文章，要懂的汉字，字数比要懂的英文为少。一百个中文字，可以组成一千三百个词语，单是成语就有一百个。用这些词语，可以组成许多不同主题的日常对话和短文。

科技越来越发达，经济、政治、社会上新生事物越来越多，新的名词必然会增加。中文占优势的地方就在于新的名词可以用旧的字组合，并不需要创造新的文字。一般人只要懂得一千个左右中文字，看书报就足够应用了。

林珊这次主编的《百字神通》(Passport to Chinese)，选出的一百字，是从四十四万个新闻用字中以电脑计算出现频率的次数，从中再选出最高频率的一百字，也就是华文中最集中、最有生命力的一百字了。"巧妇难为无米之炊",但在这里,巧妇林珊,只用一百粒米,却能烧出一道又一道的美味佳肴。这些汉字到了她手里,翻过来,倒过去,变出许多花样。比如用这一百字形容"他是个好人"可以有二十种不同的说法,至于"他是个怎样的人"就更多了,可以有九十五种。

我希望林珊这本书和类似读物的出版,能激发更多人学习华文的兴趣,以及协助有意或正在学习华文的人士,使得学习华文蔚为风气,并为促进华族语文、文化的下一阶段的工作,做出贡献。

麟记区国会议员
欧进福博士

CONTENTS

1. 100 Most Commonly Used Chinese Characters (alphabetical order based on *hanyu pinyin*)

一	二	三	四	五	六	七	八	九	十

吧	不	车	成	吃	出	从	打	大	到
道	得	的	地	点	动	都	对	多	发
分	个	工	国	过	还	好	和	很	后
候	回	会	几	己	家	见	进	经	就
开	看	可	口	来	老	了	里	么	没
们	面	明	那	你	年	起	前	情	去
人	上	少	什	时	是	事	说	他	天
头	为	我	下	现	想	小	心	行	学
样	要	也	已	以	用	有	又	在	怎
这	知	之	只	中	主	子	自	走	做

yī	èr	sān	sì	wǔ	liù	qī	bā	jiǔ	shí

ba	bù	chē	chéng	chī	chū	cóng	dǎ; dá	dà	dào
dào	dé; de; děi	de; dǐ; dī	de; dì	diǎn	dòng	dōu; dū	duì	duō	fā; fà
fēn; fèn	gè	gōng	guó	guò	hái; huán	hǎo; hào	hē; hú; huó	hěn	hòu
hòu	huí	huì	jǐ; jī	jǐ	jiā	jiàn	jìn	jīng	jiù
kāi	kān; kàn	kě	kǒu	lái	lǎo	le; liǎo	lǐ	me	méi; mò
men	miàn	míng	nà	nǐ	nián	qǐ	qián	qíng	qù
rén	shàng	shǎo; shào	shén	shí	shì	shì	shuō	tā	tiān
tóu	wéi; wèi	wǒ	xià	xiàn	xiǎng	xiǎo	xīn	xíng; háng	xué
yàng	yào	yě	yǐ	yǐ	yòng	yǒu	yòu	zài	zěn
zhè; zhèi	zhī	zhī	zhī; zhí	zhōng; zhòng	zhǔ	zǐ; zi	zì	zǒu	zuò

100 Most Commonly Used Chinese Characters (in order of frequency of use)

一	二	三	四	五	六	七	八	九	十

的	了	不	是	来	他	们	我	有	在
人	个	上	去	子	小	这	到	里	大
说	要	你	天	看	那	时	很	家	就
都	也	老	国	和	下	学	地	过	出
好	可	起	会	还	么	以	用	得	后
又	吃	多	做	见	没	年	走	打	头
事	工	成	想	开	面	动	从	心	现
车	发	只	前	回	自	对	样	道	进
中	经	点	明	行	几	为	怎	己	吧
什	知	口	候	已	分	情	主	少	之

100 Most Commonly Used Chinese Characters (according to the complexity of strokes)

一	二	三	四	五	六	七	八	九	十

人	又	几	了	大	小	个	子	上	下
口	己	已	工	么	之	也	心	中	以
为	从	不	开	车	什	见	天	少	分
他	们	用	小	发	去	对	主	可	打
出	只	年	老	多	会	有	自	动	后
回	好	地	成	吃	在	过	那	行	设
我	来	里	时	你	这	走	还	进	吧
学	现	明	和	国	的	到	经	事	知
要	面	说	很	前	是	看	点	怎	样
家	起	候	都	得	做	情	就	道	想

100 Most Commonly Used Chinese Characters (according to the structure)

Form of Structure	Example	Proportion
singular structure	一二三四五六七八九十不小少头已己也之心口来年人大天又上中下了子自见面工发开几主为车么	
top & bottom combination	里要出学去家多会是分点怎只想前个走	
top, middle & bottom combination	事	
left & right combination	从以吃和他地你们现时明好得很那都样知行吧什没对动情候就到打经说的成我	
left, middle & right combination	做	

6

Form of Structure	Example	Proportion
half covered component structure	后在看有老	
	可	
	这过进还道起	
	用	
enclosure with a component	回国	
pyramidal structure	品*	

* not included in the 100 characters

2. Basic Strokes

Stroke	、	一	丨	丿	乀
Name	dot	horizontal	vertical	downstroke to the left	downstroke to the right
Example	主	十	中	人	八

Stroke	✓	乛	乛	乛	乙
Name	tick	horizontal with downstroke to the left	horizontal with turn	horizontal hook	horizontal with turn and horizontal turn
Example	打	又	口	家	没

Stroke	乙	亅	弓	乙	弓
Name	horizontal with turn and tick	horizontal with turn and hook	horizontal with downstroke to the left and bent hook	horizontal with turn and horizontal turn with hook	horizontal with turn and turned downstroke to the left
Example	说	明	都	九	建*

Stroke	弓	乚	乚	亅	乚
Name	horizontal with turn and turned back	vertical with tick	vertical with turn	vertical hook	vertical with turn and downstroke to the left
Example	乃*	很	出	小	专*

* not included in the 100 characters.

Stroke	㇄	㇉	㇁	ㄥ	㇗
Name	vertical with turn and hook	vertical with turn and vertical turn with hook	downstroke to the left with dot	downstroke to the left with turn	bent hook
Example	几	马*	好	么	子

Stroke	㇂	㇃	辶
Name	oblique hook	reclining oblique hook	dot, horizontal with turn and turned downstroke to the left and reclining downstroke to the right
Example	我	心	过

* not included in the 100 characters.

10

3. Exercise of Basic Strokes

、									
一									
丨									
丿									
⟍									
⟋									
乛									
㇀									
一									
㇊									
㇉									
亅									

乙								
乙								
彡								
冫								
亅								
乚								
亅								
乚								
乚								
勹								
乀								
丿								
亅								
乀								
凵								
辶								

4. Hanyu Pinyin

The *pinyin* system is a phonetic scheme used in China and internationally for the romanization of the Chinese language. The table below shows the Chinese *pinyin* pronunciation with English equivalent.

Pinyin Letters		Pronunciation Equivalent		
		English	Chinese	
vowels	a	**a**h	啊	
	e	flow**er**	鹅	
	i	**i**f	衣	bi, pi, mi, di, ti, hi, li, ji, qi, xi
	o	**or**	喔	
	u	**woo**l	污	
		fee *	玉	French: tù German: Munchen
diphthong	ei	w**ay**	诶	
	ie	**yea**h	噎	
semi-vowel	w	**wo**man	污	
	y	**yi**ppie	衣	
consonant	b	**boa**r	波	
	p	**po**lar	坡	strongly aspirated

* There is no English equivalent; this is the closest in pronunciation.

consonant	m	**more**	摸	
	f	be**fore**	佛	
	d	deci**ded**	得	
	t	de**ter**	特	strongly aspirated
	n	**nur**se	呢	
	l	**l**earn	乐	
	g	**gir**l	哥	
	k	hand**ker**chief	科	
	h	**her**	喝	strongly aspirated
	j	**ji**tter	基	
	q	**chee**tah	期	
	x	**see**	西	
	z	reali**ze** *	资	
	c	ca**ts** *	雌	
	s	**si**r	思	
	zh	**g**iraffe*	知	
	ch	cat**ch** *	吃	
	sh	bu**sh***	师	
	r	inte**r**est*	日	
	v	used only for foreign words & dialects		

5. Four Tones

THE TONES — There are FOUR tones in Mandarin, and each character uses at least one fixed tone. The tone of a character changes with the meaning of the character. That is why the accurate enunciation of the tone is so important. The tones range from high to low in the following way:

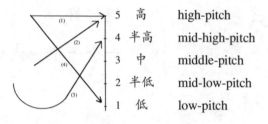

		5	高	high-pitch
(1)		4	半高	mid-high-pitch
(2)		3	中	middle-pitch
(4)		2	半低	mid-low-pitch
(3)		1	低	low-pitch

4 tones	Chinese name	tone marker	tone contour	tone value	example
T-1	high tone	ˉ	高而平 high and even		一 yī
T-2	rising tone	ˊ	由低升高 rising		国 guó
T-3	dipping tone	ˇ	由半低下降 low/long/rising		老 lǎo
T-4	falling tone	ˋ	由高降低 falling		少 shào

Neutral Tone

The tone rises and falls, become abrupt or drawn out and is stressed or unstressed. This is why Mandarin is one of the most melodious spoken languages in the world. The neutral tone is weak, unmarked. The second syllable of each of the following bisyllabic words is unmarked.

1. 好吧
2. 我的
3. 多么
4. 三个

5. 对了
6. 我们
7. 做得好
8. 一个一个地走进来

6. 100 Most Commonly Used Chinese Characters (according to the four tones)

(1) High Tone [¯]

一三七八

车吃出都 (dōu) 都 (dū) 多发 (fā) 分 (fēn) 工 几 (jī)
家经开看 (kān) 说他天心知之只 (zhī) 中 (zhōng)

(2) Rising Tone [´]

十成从打 (dá) 得 (dé) 的 (dí) 国还 (hái) 行 (háng) 还
(huán) 和 (hé) 和 (huó) 回来没明年前情人什时头为 (wéi) 行 (xíng) 学

(3) Dipping Tone [ˇ]

五九

打 (dǎ) 得 (děi) 点好 (hǎo) 很几己可口老了 (liǎo) 里你起少
(shǎo) 我想小也已以有怎只 (zhǐ) 主子走

(4) Falling Tone [`]

二四六

不大到道地 (dì) 的 (dì) 动对发 (fà) 分 (fèn) 个 (gè) 过好 (hào)
后候会见进就看 (kàn) 没 (mò) 面那去上少 (shào) 是事
为 (wèi) 下现样要用又在这中 (zhòng) 自做

(5) Neutral Tone [   ]

吧 (ba) 的 (de) 得 (de) 地 (de) 个 (ge) 和 (hu) 了 (le) 么 (me)
们 (men) 子 (zi)

17

7. Meanings of Chinese Radicals

(Radicals with their own pronunciation also function as independent characters)

人	rén	person	黾	mǐn	fly
亻		person	鹿	lù	deer
彳	chì	walk	龙	lóng	dragon
女	nǚ	female	虍		tiger
父	fù	father	角	jiǎo	horn
母	mǔ	mother	爪	zhuǎ	claw
子	zǐ	child	羽	yǔ	feather
儿	ér	child	毛	máo	hair
身	shēn	body	皮	pí	skin
自	zì	self	齿	chǐ	tooth
己	jǐ	oneself	骨	gǔ	bone
老	lǎo	old	耳	ěr	ear
士	shì	scholar	鼻	bí	nose
臣	chén	official in feudal times	目	mù	eye
			口	kǒu	mouth
牛	niú	ox	舌	shé	tongue
马	mǎ	horse	心	xīn	heart
羊	yáng	goat	忄		heart
豕	shǐ	pig	手	shǒu	hand
		cat	扌		hand
豸		animal	足	zú	foot
犭			走	zǒu	walk
犬	quǎn	dog	辶		to run
鼠	shǔ	mouse	舟	zhōu	boat
鸟	niǎo	bird	车	chē	vehicle
虫	chóng	insect	戈	gē	dagger-axe
鱼	yú	fish			

矛	máo	spear	全	jīn	gold
弓	gōng	bow	玉	yù	jade
刀	dāo	knife	木	mù	timber
刂		knife	禾	hé	grain
矢	shǐ	arrow	艹		grass
革	gé	leather	竹		bamboo
斤	jīn	kati	纟		silk
瓦	wǎ	tile	衣	yī	cloth
缶	fǒu	jar	衤		cloth
臼	jiū	mortar	礻		God
米	mǐ	rice	门	mén	door
麦	mài	wheat	户	hù	door
瓜	guā	melon	尸	shī	corpse
豆	dòu	bean	阝		city
谷	gǔ	grain	厂	chǎng	factory
麻	má	gunny	广	guǎng	broad
饣	shí	food	疒		sickness
日	rì	sun	大	dà	big
月	yuè	moon; flesh	小	xiǎo	small
夕	xī	night	贝	bèi	shell; money
风	fēng	wind	见	jiàn	see
雨	yǔ	rain	乙	yǐ	second
水	shuǐ	water	又	yòu	again
氵		water	力	lì	force
冫		ice	巾	jīn	scarf
火	huǒ	fire	韦	wěi	leather
灬		fire	方	fāng	square
气	qì	air	斗	dǒu	a measure for grain
山	shān	mountain			
田	tián	field	文	wén	script
土	tǔ	earth	攵		script
石	shí	stone	欠	qiàn	owe

19

言	yán	word	鬼	guǐ	ghost
讠		word	血	xiě	blood
音	yīn	sound	皿	mǐn	container
页	yè	page	西	xī	west
业	yè	job	酉	yǒu	a period of time
立	lì	stand	辰	chén	a period of time
工	gōng	work	疋	pǐ	a classifier
寸	cùn	inch	青	qīng	green
止	zhǐ	stop	、		dot
赤	chì	red	一		horizontal stroke
佳	jiā	good	二		dot and horizontal stroke
其	qí	that			horizontal stroke
片	piàn	piece	丨		vertical stroke
采	cǎi	pluck	丿		left falling stroke
比	bǐ	compare	二	èr	two
歹	dǎi	bad	八	bā	eight
里	lǐ	inside; a Chinese unit of length	十	shí	ten
			凵		hollow
辛	xīn	hard	囗		enclose
用	yòng	use	冖		cover
卤	lǔ	salt	宀		roof
黑	hēi	black	卜		divination
白	bái	white	穴	xué	cave

20

8. Exercise on 50 Commonly Used Radicals

(1) **2 strokes** ノ 亻 rén person

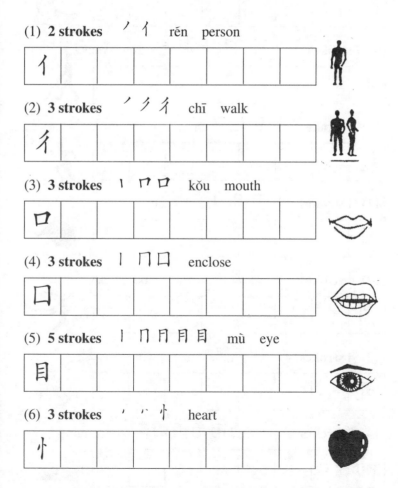

(2) **3 strokes** ノ ク 彳 chī walk

(3) **3 strokes** l 冂 口 kǒu mouth

(4) **3 strokes** l 冂 口 enclose

(5) **5 strokes** l 冂 冃 月 目 mù eye

(6) **3 strokes** ノ ν 忄 heart

(7) **3 strokes**   一 十 才   hand

才							

(8) **7 strokes**   丶 ㅁ ㅁ ㅁ ㅂ ㅂ ㅂ 足   zú foot

足							

(9) **7 strokes**   一 十 土 キ 丰 走 走   zǒu walk

走							

(10) **3 strokes**   丶 亠 辶   run

辶							

(11) **4 strokes**   丨 冂 冃 日   rì sun

日							

(12) **4 strokes**   丿 刀 月 月   yuè moon; flesh

月							

(13) **4 strokes**   丿 几 凡 风   fēng wind

风							

(14) **8 strokes**   一 亅 冂 雨 雨 雨 雨 雨   yǔ rain

雨							

(15) **2 strokes** 丶 冫 ice

冫							

(16) **3 strokes** 丶 冫 氵 water

氵							

(17) **4 strokes** 丿 𠂉 𠂉 气 qì air

气							

(18) **4 strokes** 丶 丷 灱 火 huǒ fire

火							

(19) **3 strokes** 丿 𠂉 饣 shí food

饣							

(20) **2 strokes** 丶 讠 word

讠							

(21) **3 strokes** 一 十 土 tǔ earth

土							

(22) **5 strokes** 一 丆 石 石 石 shí stone

石							

(23) **5 strokes** ノ 𠂉 𠂉 乍 钅 jīn metal

钅							

(24) **4 strokes** 一 二 千 王（玉 yù jade）

王							

(25) **4 strokes** 一 十 才 木 mù wood

木							

(26) **5 strokes** 一 二 千 禾 禾 hé grain

禾							

(27) **3 strokes** 一 十 艹 grass

艹							

(28) **6 strokes** ノ 𠂉 𠂉 𣥂 竹 竹 bamboo

竹							

(29) **6 strokes** 丶 口 口 中 虫 虫 chóng insect

虫							

(30) **3 strokes** ノ 犭 犭 animal

犭							

(31) **3 strokes** 　人 女 女　nǚ　female

女							

(32) **3 strokes** 　ㄥ 幺 纟　silk

纟							

(33) **5 strokes** 　丶 亠 礻 衤 衤　clothing

衤							

(34) **4 strokes** 　丶 亠 ネ 礻　god

礻							

(35) **3 strokes** 　丶 丷 宀　roof

宀							

(36) **2 strokes** 　丶 冖　cover

冖							

(37) **3 strokes** 　丶 冂 门　mén　door

门							

(38) **2 strokes** 　㇇ 阝　city

阝							

(39) **3 strokes** `丶 亠 广` guǎng broad

广						

(40) **5 strokes** `丶 亠 广 疒 疒` disease

疒						

(41) **3 strokes** `丨 屮 山` shān mountain

山						

(42) **5 strokes** `丨 冂 日 田 田` tián field

田						

(43) **6 strokes** `丶 丷 亠 半 米 米` mǐ rice

米						

(44) **5 strokes** `丿 勹 勺 鸟 鸟` niǎo bird

鸟						

(45) **8 strokes** `丿 勹 勺 勺 甸 甸 鱼 鱼` yú fish

鱼						

(46) **2 strokes** `丨 刂` knife

刂						

(47) **3 strokes** 一 ナ 大　dà　big

大						

(48) **3 strokes** 亅 小 小　xiǎo　small

小						

(49) **4 strokes** 丨 冂 贝 贝　bèi　shell

贝						

(50) **4 strokes** 丨 冂 见 见　jiàn　see

见						

9. Numerical Figures

Chinese numerical figures are simple, interesting and useful. Only 15 characters are needed to spell out any amount in figures. They are: yi, er, san, si, wu, liu, qi, ba, jiu, shi, ling, together with four quantity measure words of bai, qian, wan, yi.

Eg. For big figures like 987,654,321, the Chinese reads:
     jiu yi ba qian qi bai liu shi wu wan si qian san bai er shi yi.

Eg. Decimal: 123.075, the Chinese reads:
     yi bai er shi san dian ling qi wu

Eg. Fraction: 4089/36257, the Chinese read:
     san wan liu qian er bai wu shi qi fen zhi si qian ling ba shi jiu

Eg. Proportion: 59:72, the Chinese reads:
     wu shi jiu bi qi shi er

We need only these 15 figures to express everything in numerics. If we use English, 32 different words are needed, because of irregular cases. For example:

(1) three
(2) thirteen
(3) thirty

All of these three words are different. In Chinese 十三 (shi san) becomes 三十 (san shi) when the two words are reversed. All we need are just the two words 'san' and 'shi' for the three words.

The months of a year and days of the week are numbered in order and no special terms are needed.

Eg. yi yue (January), er yue (February) ... shi er yue (December); xing qi yi (Monday) ... xing qi liu (Saturday).

Usage

一五一十	(to narrate) systematically and in full detail
二心	disloyalty
三三五五	in threes and fours
四面	four sides
五行	the five elements (metal, wood, water, fire and earth)
六经	the *Six Classics*
七七八八	70 to 80 per cent completed
八成	80 per cent
九天	the Ninth Heaven; the highest of heavens
十之八九	most likely

10. Usage of 100 Most Commonly Used Chinese Characters

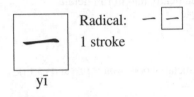

Radical: 一 一

1 stroke

yī

Meanings and examples

(1) one; first: 一个人 a person; (一) firstly

(2) full; all: 一行 (xíng) 人 a group of people

一成*	ten per cent
一打 (dā)*	a dozen
一道	together; side by side; alongside
一点*	a little; a dot; one o'clock
一点小事	a small matter
一动	easily; frequently; at every turn
一对*	a pair; a couple
一二	one or two; just; a few; just a little
一分*	a cent
一分为二	one divided into two
一个*	a
一个也不少	not even one is missing
一行 (háng)*	a line
一回*	a chapter; once; one round

一回事	a thing; a matter
一会	a little while
一己	oneself
一家*	a household; a school of thought
一家大小	the young and old in a family
一家和好	a family in harmony
一经	as soon as; at once
一…就…	no sooner…than…; the moment…
一口*	a mouthful; a bite; with certainty; classifier for pig
一来一去	in the course of contacts
一面*	one side; one aspect
一面…一面	at the same time
一年到头	throughout the year; all year round
一起	in the same place; together; altogether
一前一后	front and back
一人*	a person
一时*	a period of time; for a short while; temporary
一事	be related (organizationally or professionally); belonging to the same organization
一天*	a day; one day; the whole day
一头*	directly; headlong; classifier for cow, pig, goat and deer
一五一十	(to narrate) systematically and in full detail
一下*	one time; once; in a short while
一心	wholeheartedly; heart and soul; of one mind
一行 (xíng)	a group travelling together; a party
一样	the same; equally; alike; as…as…
一一	one by one; one after another

一只 (zhī)*   an (animal)

一走了(liǎo)之 to evade a problem

* can be interchangeable with other numbers

Radical: 一 　一 二

2 strokes

èr

Meanings and examples

(1) two; second: 一二三 one, two, three

(2) different: 二心 disloyalty or halfheartedness

二地主   sub-landlord

二分点   the equinoxes

二心   disloyalty; halfheartedness

Radical: 一 　一 二 三

3 strokes

sān

Meaning and example

(1) three; third: 三行 (háng) three rows

三国   the Three Kingdoms (220–280), namely Wei (220
　　　　　　–265), Shu Han (221–263) and Wu (222–280)

三九天   the third nine-day period after the winter solstice
　　　　　　— the coldest days of winter

三七   pseudo-ginseng

三七开   a seventy-thirty ratio

三三五五   in threes and fours

Radical: 口 丨 冂 冂 四 四

5 strokes

sì

Meaning and example

(1) four; fourth: 四面 four sides

四国 Shikoku, Japan

四面 four sides; all sides

四起 rising from all directions

四时 the four seasons

四下里 all around

Radical: 一 一 丁 五 五

4 strokes

wǔ

Meaning and example

(1) five; fifth: 五个小时 five hours

五经 *the Five Classics*, namely, *The Book of Songs, The Books of History, The Book of Changes, The Book of Rites* and *The Spring and Autumn Annals*

五行 (xíng) the five elements (metal, wood, water, fire and earth)

六
liù

Radical: 一 丶 亠 六

4 strokes

Meaning and example

(1) six; sixth: 六年 six years

六经   *the Six Classics, namely, The Book of Songs, The Book of History, The Book of Changes, The Book of Rites, The Spring and Autumn Annals, and The Rites of Zhou*

七
qī

Radical: 一 一 七

2 strokes

Meaning and example

(1) seven; seventh: 七天 seven days

七七八八	70 to 80 per cent completed
七情	the seven human emotions, namely joy, anger, sorrow, fear, love, hate and desire
七上八下	be agitated; be perturbed
七十二 行 (háng)	all sorts of occupations; every conceivable field of work
七老八十	about 70 to 80 years old; very old

Radical: 八 丿 八
2 strokes

bā

Meaning and example

(1) eight; eighth: 八分 eight cents

八成　　　eighty per cent; most probably
八小时工　eight-hour work/job

Radical: 丿 丿 九
2 strokes

jiǔ

Meaning and example

(1) nine; ninth: 九时 nine o'clock

九天　　　the Ninth Heaven; the highest of heavens

Radical: 十 一 十
2 strokes

shí

Meanings and examples

(1) ten; tenth: 十国 ten countries
(2) topmost: 十成 100 per cent

十二分　　more than 100 per cent; extremely
十分　　　very; fully; utterly; extremely; ten cents

"十三点"	scatter-brain and unsteady
十·一	October 1, National day of the People's Republic of China
十之八九	most likely

吧
ba

Radical: 口
7 strokes

丨 口 口 口ㄱ 口ㄱㄱ 口ㄲ 吧

Meanings and examples

(1) to show that one is making a guess or asking question: 你会做吧？ You can do it, can't you?
(2) to show that one is asking for another's view: 我们一起走吧！ Let's go together.
(3) to show that one is giving command: 进来吧！ Come in! 你好好想想吧！ You'd better think it over carefully. 说吧！ Speak up! 走吧！ Let's go!
(4) to show that one is agreeable: 好吧！ All right! 就这样吧！ Let it be! 就这么做吧！ All right, let's do it this way!

不
bù

Radical: 一
4 strokes

一 プ プ 不

Meaning and example

(1) to indicate negative or opposite meaning: 不好 no good; 不对 wrong

不成	can't; won't do
不大	not very…; unlikely
不大不小	neither big nor small
不得	can't; may not; mustn't
不得不	have no choice but to; have to
不得了 (liǎo)	desperately serious; extremely

不得人心	unpopular; doesn't enjoy popular support
不得已	have no alternative but to; act against one's will
不对/不对头	wrong
不多	not many; not much
不多见	rare
不过	but; only; no more than
不好	no good
不好吃*	not delicious
不和	doesn't get along well (with somebody); on bad terms
不会	unable to; won't
不会走*	can't go or walk
不见	not see; disappear
不见得	not necessarily; not likely; doesn't seem; doesn't appear
不见了	disappear; be missing
不可/不可以	can't
不可多得	rare; hard to come by
不可回头	can't turn back; irrevocable
不可以吃*	can't eat
不了 (liǎo)	without end; not finish
不了 (liǎo) 了 (liǎo) 之	inconclusive; end up with nothing definite
不了 (liǎo) 情	everlasting love
不明	not clear; unknown; fail to understand
不情	presumptuous; unreasonable
不人道	inhuman
不三不四	dubious; shady

不上不下	stuck in between
不少	many
不时	frequently; at any time
不是	no; not; fault
不是时候	not the right time; untimely
不为	not do
不想	don't want
不想吃*	don't want to eat
不行 (xíng)	won't do; doesn't work
不行(xíng)了	can't make it; can't survive it
不要	don't
不要吃*	don't eat
不一	not the same; differ
不一样	not the same kind
不已	endlessly; incessantly
不用	needn't; unnecessary
不在	be out; not here
不在家	not at home
不在了	be dead
不怎么	not very; not particularly
不怎么样	of no consequence; does not matter much; very indifferent
不知	unknowingly
不只	not only; not merely
不中 (zhòng)	guess wrongly; can't hit the target
不中用	unfit for anything; of no good; useless
不走	not go

*can be used interchangeably with other verbs.

Radical: 车 一 圡 卡 车

4 strokes

车 chē

Meanings and examples

(1) vehicle or machine: 大车 big vehicle/heavy vehicle
(2) chariot: 车 (jū) one of the pieces in Chinese chess

车道	(traffic) lane
车工	sewing worker; tailoring
车后	behind a car
车前	in front of a car
车上	on the vehicle
车头	bonnet of car
车子	small vehicle; car

Radical: 戊 一 厂 厂 成 成 成

6 strokes

成 chéng

Meanings and examples

(1) accomplish: 事成之后 after the achievement of something

(2) turn into 成为

成分	composition; ingredient; one's status
成家	(of a man) get married
成见	prejudice
成就	achievement; accomplishment

40

成年	grow up; adult; year after year
成人	grow up; adult
成事	accomplish something; succeed
成说	accepted theory or concept
成天	all the time; all day long
成为	become; turn into
成心	intentionally

Radical: 口   丨 冂 口 口ノ 口レ 吃

6 strokes

chī

Meanings and examples

(1) eat; take: 吃点心 have some refreshments
(2) food 吃的

吃不得	can be eaten; can't afford to eat
吃不开	be unpopular; won't work
吃不来	dislike certain food
吃不上	be unable to get something to eat; miss a meal
吃不下	having no appetite; be unable to eat any more
吃得	eat to the degree that…
吃得多	eat a lot
吃得开	be popular; be much sought after
吃得来	be able to eat; not mind eating
吃得上	can afford to eat; be able to get a meal
吃得少	eat very little
吃得下	be able to eat

吃过了	have eaten
吃好了	have eaten
吃了	ate
吃人	exploit; take advantage of

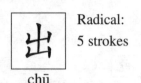

出

chū

Radical: 中

5 strokes

Meanings and examples

(1) go or come out: 出去 go out
(2) put up; issue: 出点子 offer advice
(3) attend; go to: 出工 go to work
(4) a dramatic piece: 一出 a (play)

出车	despatch a vehicle
出点子	offer advice
出动	set out; start off
出发	set out; start off; start from
出工	go to work; show up for work
出国	go abroad
出家	become a monk or nun
出家人	monk or nun
出口	speak; utter; exit; export
出来	come out; emerge
出面	act in one's own capacity or on behalf of an organization

出没 (mò)	appear and disappear; haunt
出去	go out; get out
出人头地	stand out among one's fellows
出事	meet with a mishap; have an accident
出头	lift one's head; come forward; a little over
出现	appear; emerge
出走	leave; run away; flee

Radical: 人 丿 人 从 从

4 strokes

cóng

Meanings and examples

(1) from: 从现在起 from now on
(2) ever: 从不 never
(3) follow: 从人 follower

从不	never
从来	always; at all times
从前	before; in the past
从人	follower
从上到下	from top to bottom
从事	be engaged in
从头	from the beginning
从头来过	once again
从头做起	do from the beginning
从小	from childhood
从这	from this
从中	from among; out of

Radical: 扌 一 十 扌 打

5 strokes

打
dǎ ; dá

Meanings and examples

(1) knock; hit: 打 (dǎ) 人 hit someone
(2) break: 打 (dǎ) 了 break (egg)
(3) dozen: 一打 (dá) a dozen

打不到	can't hit; miss
打道	clear the way
打点	get ready; get through
打动	move; touch
打到	hit
打发	send; despatch
打过	fought or hit
打开	open; unfold; turn on
打开来	open up
打那时起	from that time onwards
打起来	start a fight
打人	hit someone
打天下	conquer the country; establish one's career
打头	take the lead
打样	draw a design; make a proof
打这走	this way
打中	hit the mark

Radical: 大 [一 ナ 大]

3 strokes

dà

Meanings and examples

(1) big; large: 大国 big country
(2) ranked number one: 老大 eldest child or the chief

大不了	at the worst; serious
大车	cart; chief engineer (of a ship)
大吃 …	eat extravagantly…
大大/大大 地(de)	greatly
大大小小	big and small
大道	highway; avenue
大地	earth
大都 (dōu)	mostly; almost
大都 (dōu) 会	for the most part; mostly
大都 (dū) 会	big city; metropolis
大多	majority; most of
大个的	the big one
大个子	a tall person
大国	big country or power
大过	serious offence; bigger than
大好	very good; excellent
大后年	three years from now
大后天	three days from now
大会	conference; mass rally

大家	everybody; all; an authority (on a skill)
大家想想	everybody thinks
大开	open widely
大口	big mouth; big opening
大面子	great reputation
大年	good year; bumper year; a Chinese calendar year in which the last month has 30 days
大前年	three years ago
大前天	three days ago
大人	adult; father; Your Excellency
大事	important matter; great event
大事不好	a disaster is imminent; the situation is bad
大头	the bigger end; main part; silver coins which bear the image of President Yuan Shikai
大我	the respectful term referring to a group of which one is a member
大小	of varying sizes; big or small; adults and children
大学	university
大样	detail drawing
大要	main point; gist
大有可为	be well worth doing; have bright prospects
大有人在	there're plenty of such people

Radical: 至

一 工 工 五 五 至 到 到

8 strokes

dào

Meanings and examples

(1) go to: 到他家 so to his house
(2) arrive; reach: 到家 arrive at home

到过	have been to (somewhere)
到会	attend a meeting
到家	arrive at home; reach a very high level
到来	arrival
到了	arrived; reached
到了没有	has arrived or not
到那里去	go there
到时	when it's due; when it's time
到头	to the end; at an end
到头来	in the end; finally
到这里来	come here

Radical: 辶

丶 丷 ⺍ 半 首 首 首 首 首 首 道 道

12 strokes

dào

Meanings and examples

(1) road; way; path: 小道 a path
(2) say 说道
(3) classifier for door, wall and bridge: 一道 a (door)

道地	genuine; real
道行 (héng)	skill and ability
道家	Taoist school (a school of thought in the Spring and Autumn and Warring States Periods, 770-221 B.C.); Taoists
道口	road junction; level crossing
道情	chanting folk tales to the accompaniment of simple percussion instruments
道人	a respectful form of address for Taoist priests
道学	a school of Confucian philosophy in the Song Dynasty (960-1279); affectedly moral

Radical: 彳　 ′ ′ 彳 彳 彳 彳 彳 彳 彳 得 得

11 strokes

dé; de; děi

Meanings and examples

(1) get; obtain; gain 得 (dé) 到
(2) fit; proper: 得 (dé) 用 fit for use
(3) used after the verb to show the depth of the action: 说 得 (de) 不好 didn't say well
(4) need; must: 这事得 (děi) 他做主。 This matter has to be decided by him.

得出	reach (a conclusion); obtain (a result)
得到	get; obtain; gain
得分	score
得过	won; got
得以	so that…can…
得用	fit for use

Radical: 白
8 strokes

′ ⺈ ⺈ 白 白 白′ 的 的

的

de; dí; dì

Meanings and examples

(1) possessive to show whose ownership: 你的 (de) your or yours; 你们的 your or yours (plural); 你的主人 your master; 什么的 of what; 他的 his; 他们的 their or theirs; 我的 my or mine; 我们的 our or ours

(2) adjective, to describe something: 好的 (de) good; 老的 old; 小的 young

(3) emphasize, always used at the end of the sentence: 好的(de) all right; 是的 yes; 是我做的 I did it; 他说他的，我做我的。 Let him say what he wishes but I'll do what I wish.

(4) gerund, used after the verb: 开车的 (de) driver

(5) to show different actions or different ways: 说的 (de) 说，做的做。 There are those who just talk about it and those who will do the work.

(6) target: 中 (zhòng) 的 (dì) hit the target

Radical: 土
6 strokes

一 十 土 圵 坷 地

地

de; dì

Meanings and examples

(1) adverb equivalent: 用心地 (de) 学 concentrate on learning; 小心地做事 doing things carefully

(2) the earth; land; fields; ground: 大地 (dì) the earth; 工地 worksite

(3) place; position; situation: 到一地 (dì) arrive at a place

(4) distance: 走了一里地 (dì) walk for a *li* (Chinese unit of length ≐ ¹/₂ km)

地大人少	a vast but scarcely populated expanse of land
地道	tunnel; genuine; pure
地点	place; site; locale
地动	earthquake
地对地	ground-to-ground; surface-to-surface
地里	in the field
地面	the earth's surface; ground; floor; area
地上	on the ground
地头	edge of a field; the place
地下	underground; secret (activity); on the ground
地心	the earth's core
地主	landlord; host

Radical: 灬

| 丨 | ├ | 上 | 占 | 占 | 卢 | 点 | 点 | 点 |

9 strokes

diǎn

Meanings and examples

(1) drop; spot; point; dot: 三点五 three point five; 一个点 a dot
(2) a little; some: 有一点 there's some
(3) feature: 有几点要说 a few points to say
(4) hint: 一点就明白 get the hint quickly
(5) o'clock: 七点 seven o'clock
(6) refreshments 点心

点明	point out
点头	nod one's head

点心   snacks; refreshments
点子   dot; idea

Radical: 力 ｜ 一 二 云 云 云 动

6 strokes

dòng

Meanings sand examples

(1) move; act: 动了 get moving
(2) start: 动工 start building or work

动不得   can't be moved or touched (because of danger)

动不动   easily; frequently; at every turn

动不了   can't move

动工   start building or work

动情   get worked up; have one's (sexual) passions aroused

动人   moving; touching

动人的事   a stirring deed

动心   one's mind is perturbed; one's desire, enthusiasm or interest is aroused

动用   put to use; employ

Radical: 阝 一 十 土 耂 者 者 者 都 都

10 strokes

dōu; dū

Meanings and examples

(1) all; even: 都 (dōu) 有 exists for all
(2) to emphasize: 都 (dōu) 八点了 already 8 o'clock
(3) capital; big city: 都 (dū) 会 metropolis

都八十了	already 80
都吃了	everyone has eaten; everything has been eaten
都到了	all have arrived
都对	they're all correct
都好了	everything is fine now; ready
都会	be able to do all
都进过	have entered all
都看了	have seen all
都可以	all will do
都来了	all have come
都没有	nobody has
都是你	it is all because of you
都说不出	none can be expressed; nobody can express something
都说了	have said everything
都想	everybody thinks/wants
都学过	have learned all
都有用	they're all useful
都走了	everybody has left
都 (dū) 会	city; metropolis

对

duì

Radical: 又　　フ　又　又ˇ　对　对

5 strokes

Meanings and examples

(1) correct; right: 你说得对。 You've said correctly.
(2) opposite: 对面 face to face
(3) towards: 对我说 said to me
(4) treat; counter: 对人对事 treatment of people and things
(5) a pair 一对

对不对	right or not
对不起	sorry; excuse me
对得起	not let somebody down; treat somebody fairly
对打	play or fight against
对过	opposite; across the way
对己对人	unto myself and others
对开	divide into two halves; run from opposite directions
对看	vis-a-vis; face each other
对口	two performers speak or sing alternately
对面	opposite; face to face
对人	dealing with people; unto people
对事	attend to the matters
对头	correct; normal; enemy; opponent
对子	a pair of antithetical phrases

Radical: 夕　夕 ／ ク タ タ 多 多

6 strokes

duō

Meanings and examples

(1) many; much; more: 事情很多 a lot of things (matters) to attend to
(2) excessive or too much: 多好 how nice
(3) to ask about the size or degree: 多少 how much; how many

多吃	eat more
多大	how big
多多少少	more or less
多国	many countries
多过	more than
多家	many (organizations)
多看	see more
多口	more than two performers speaking or singing
多么	how; what
多面	many sides
多年	many years
多年来	over the years
多情	full of tenderness or affection
多少	amount; somewhat; how many; how much; more or less
多时	a long time
多事	meddlesome; eventful
多说	more say
多头	bull; long; multi-head

54

多想	give it more thought
多小	how small
多心	oversensitive; suspicious
多行 (xíng)	very capable
多学	learn more
多样	many kinds
多用	use more often
多做	do more; do extra work

Radical: 又 ㇐ 𠂇 ㇒ 发 发

5 strokes

fā; fà

Meanings and examples

(1) develop; expand: 面发 (fā) 起来 the dough has risen
(2) give; issue 发 (fā) 出
(3) hair 头发 (fà)

发出	issue; send out; give out
发动	launch; start; mobilize
发还 (huán)	return; give back
发家	build up a family fortune
发面	leaven dough
发明	invention
发明家	inventor
发起	initiate; launch; sponsor
发起国	sponsor nation
发起人	sponsor; initiator

发情	have one's (sexual) passions aroused
发现	find; discover
发行 (xíng)	issue; publish; distribute; put on sale
发作	break out; show effect; have a fit of anger

Radical: 八 | 丿 八 今 分

4 strokes

fēn; fèn

Meanings and examples

(1) divide; separate; part: 分 (fēn) 家 divide up family property and live apart
(2) component; what is within one's rights or duty: 过分 (fèn) exceeding what is proper; going too far
(3) fraction: 三分 (fēn) 之二 two-thirds

分道	alley; separate
分发	issue; distribute; hand out
分工	divide the work; division of labour
分行 (háng)	branch (of a bank or a company)
分会	branch (of a society, committee, association)
分家	divide up family property and live apart; break up the family and live apart
分开	separate; part
分明	clearly demarcated; sharply contoured; distinct
分说	defend oneself (against a charge); explain matters
分头	separately

分心	distract one's attention
分 (fēn) 子	numerator; molecule
分 (fèn) 子	member; element

Radical: 人 ｜ ノ 人 个

3 strokes

gè

Meaning and example

(1) classifier for most of the nouns used without specific classifier: 一个人 a man; 这个 this one; 那个 that one

个个	each and every one; all
个个一样	all are the same
个人	individual; I (pronoun)
个头	size; height
个头不小	not of a small size
个中	therein
个中人	a person in the know
个子	height; build
个子大	of big build
个子小	of small build

工

gōng

Radical: 工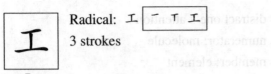

3 strokes

Meanings and examples

(1) work; production: 做工 work
(2) industry 工业
(3) worker 工人

工地	worksite; construction site
工分 (fēn)	merit point for work (a unit indicating the quantity and quality of labour performed, and the amount of payment earned)
工会	trade union; labour union
工人	worker; workman
工时	man-hour
工事	fortifications; defence work
工头	foreman

国

guó

Radical: 口

8 strokes

Meanings and examples

(1) country; state; nation 国家
(2) of the nation; national: 国家大事 national affairs

国都 (dū)	national capital
国会	parliament

国家	country; state; nation
国家大事	national or state affairs
国家学说	theory of the state
国情	condition of a country
国人	compatriots; fellow countrymen
国事	national or state affairs
国学	studies of Chinese ancient civilization (including philosophy, history, archaeology, literature, linguistics, etc.)
国有	nationalized; belong to the state

过

guò

Radical: 辶　一 十 寸 寸 讨 过

6 strokes

Meanings and examples

(1) cross; pass: 从我家过 pass by my house
(2) over; after: 过了几天 after a few days
(3) mistake; fault: 大过 serious offence
(4) finished: 吃过 already eaten

过不了三天	can't last for three days; not more than three days
过不去	can't get over; make it difficult for; sorry
过从	have friendly interaction; associate
过道	passageway; corridor
过得	the way of getting by or spending one's life
过得去	can get by; not so bad
过多	too much

过分 (fēn)	over the limit; unduly excessive
过后	later on; afterwards
过来	come over
过来看	come over and see
过来人	a person who has had the experience
过了	passed; past
过年	celebrate the New Year; after this year
过去	in or of the past; formerly; go over; pass by
过去了 (le)	pass away
过人	surpass; better than others
过时	out-of-date; obsolete
过头	go beyond the limit; overdo; excessive

Radical: 辶

一 丆 才 不 不 讠丕 还

7 strokes

hái; huán

Meanings and examples

(1) still; yet: 他还 (hái) 好。 He's still fine.
(2) even more: 他做得比我还 (hái) 要好。 He does even
    better than me.
(3) return; back: 还 (huán) 你 return to you; 还 (huán) 家 return
    home

还不回来	yet to return
还好 (hǎo)	not bad; fortunately; tolerable
还可以	can do; tolerable
还没有	still not
还没吃过	have yet to eat

还是	still; nevertheless; had better; or
还要	want or needed again
还有	still have; still available
还在	still there; still exist
还 (huán) 家	return home
还 (huán) 口	answer back

Radical: 女 ㄥ ㄥ 女 女 好 好

6 strokes

hǎo; hào

Meanings and examples

(1) good; fine; nice: 好事 good deeds
(2) very; how: 好大 very big
(3) finished; completed 做好了
(4) easy to do 好做
(5) like; be fond of: 好 (hào) 学 eager to learn

好不	how (to indicate degree); so
好吃	delicious
好大	very big
好多	a good many
好多了	much better (recover)
好过	have an easy time; better than
好好的(hǎo hāo de)	in good condition
好好地 (hǎo hāo de) 想一想	think it over carefully

好看	good-looking; nice; interesting; honoured; proud
好了	recover; become friends again
好人	good person
好事	good deed; an act of charity
好说	well said or spoken
好天	fine day; fine weather
好心	good intention; kind-hearted
好样的	fine example; great fellow
好一个…	what a nice or good…
好用	easy to use
好在	fortunately; luckily
好走	smooth or easy for walking
好吃*	be fond of eating
好动*	active; restless
好事*	meddlesome; officious
好事的人*	busybody
好学*	eager to learn

*好 pronounced hào

 Radical: 禾   ノ ニ 千 千 禾 禾 和 和

8 strokes

hé; hú; huó

Meanings and examples

(1) and: 你和他 you and he
(2) harmonious; on good terms: 不和 on bad terms
(3) peace: 说和 mediate a settlement

(4) sum: 二三之和 sum of two and three
(5) mix with water: 和 (huó) 面 knead doughs
(6) meet the requirement for and win the mahjong or card game
和(hú)

和好	become reconciled
和会	peace conference
和事老	peacemaker
和 (huó) 面	knead dough

Radical: 彳

', ' 彳 彳 彳 彳 彳 很 很 很

9 strokes

hěn

Meaning and example

(1) very; quite: 好得很 very good

很不好	very bad
很大	very big
很对	quite correct
很多	many; quite a lot; a great deal
很多国家	many countries
很多年	many years
很多人	many people
很多事	a lot of things or matters
很多天	many days
很好	very good
很好看	good-looking; very beautiful
很看不起	look down upon very much
很看得起	think very highly

很老	very old
很想	wishes or desires to do something
很小	very small
很行 (xíng)	capable; competent
很有见地	have keen insight; show good judgement
很有用	very useful

Radical: 厂   ´ 厂 厂 斤 后 后

6 strokes

hòu

Meanings and examples

(1) back; behind; rear: 车后 behind the car
(2) after; later: 他先来，我后到。 He came first and I came later.
(3) offspring: 后人 descendants

后进	lagging behind; less advanced; backward
后来	afterward; later
后来人	successors
后面	behind; later; at the back
后年	the year after next
后起	of the younger generation
后人	later generations; descendants
后事	what happened afterwards; funeral affairs
后天	day after tomorrow; postnatal
后头	at the back; later
后学	pupil of a young age

Radical: 亻
10 strokes

丿 亻 亻 伫 伫 伊 伊 侯 侯 候

hòu

Meanings and examples

(1) wait; await: 候车 waiting for a vehicle
(2) time 时候
(3) send regards: 问候 send one's regards
(4) weather 天候

候车 waiting for a vehicle

Radical: 口
6 strokes

丨 冂 冂 冋 冋 回

huí

Meanings and examples

(1) return; go back: 回家 go/come home
(2) reply; answer: 回信 send a letter in reply
(3) classifier for events, incidents or actions: 他来过这里三回。
He has been here thrice. 这是怎么一回事？ What's the
matter?
(4) chapter: 一回 a chapter

回不来   can't go back
回不回去   whether to go back or not
回到家   reach home
回动   reverse
回国   return to one's country

回家	return home
回见	see you later/again
回来	come back; return
回去	go back; return; back
回人	the Hui nationality in China
回头	later; repent; turn one's head; look back
回头见	see you later
回想	recall; recollect

会

Radical: 人 丿 亽 亼 会 会 会

6 strokes

huì

Meanings and examples

(1) assemble; get together: 开会 hold a meeting
(2) association; society; union: 工会 trade union
(3) can; be able to; understand; know: 我会做。 I can (modal) do; 你很会吃。 You know what's good to eat.
(4) meet; see: 会见 meet with

会不会	can or not
会打到人	can hit the people
会得 (dé) 到	can get; can achieve
会动	mobile; movable
会见	meet with
会看	able to read
会面	meet
会上	at the meeting
会想	able to think; sensible

66

| 会心 | of understanding; of knowing |
| 会学人家 | able to imitate |

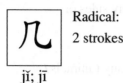

Radical: 几 丿 几

2 strokes

jǐ; jī

Meanings and examples

(1) small table 几 (jī)
(2) how many: 要几 (jǐ) 天? How many days are needed?
(3) a few: 过几 (jǐ) 天 after a few days; 十几天 more than ten days

几打 (dǎ)	a few dozens; How many dozens?
几点	a few points; What time?
几对	a few pairs/couples; How many pairs/couples?
几分	a bit; rather; somewhat; a few marks/cents; How many marks/cents?
几个	several (things); How many (things)?
几国	a few countries; How many countries?
几行 (háng)	a few lines; How many lines?
几回	a few chapters/times; How many chapters/times?
几家	a few households; How many households?
几口	a few bites; a few (pigs)
几里	a few *li*; How many *li*?
几面	a few sides; How many sides?
几年	a few years; How many years?
几起	a few (cases); How many (cases)?

几个人	a few people; How many people?
几时	When; What time?
几天	a few days; How many days?
几头	a few sides or aspects; How many sides or aspects?
几样	a few kind; How many kinds?
几只	a few (animals / things); How many (animals / things)?

Radical: 己　　己 コ 己

3 strokes

jǐ

Meaning and example

(1) oneself; personal: 自己 self

己见　　personal opinion; one's own view

Radical: 宀　　丶 ヽ 宀 宀 宀 宀 宀 宀 宀 家 家

10 strokes

jiā

Meanings and examples

(1) family; household: 我家 my family
(2) specialist: 小说家 novelist

家道	family financial circumstance
家国	family and nation
家和	a family in harmony; peace in a family

68

家家	every household; each family
家口	members of a family; the number of people in a family
家里	in a house or family
家人	members of a family
家事	family matters; domestic affairs
家小	wife and children
家学	knowledge passed from generation to generation in a family
家用	family expenses; housekeeping money
家有一老	there's an old person in the family
家中	at home; in the family

Radical: 见 | 丨 冂 见 见 |

4 strokes

jiàn

Meanings and examples

(1) see: 我见到他。 I've seen him.
(2) meet with: 我不要见他。 I don't want to meet him.
(3) view; opinion: 我之见 my opinion

见不到	don't meet; can't see/meet
见不得 (de)	not to be exposed to
见不得 (de) 人	not fit to be seen or revealed; shameful
见得 (de)	seem; appear
见地 (dì)	insight; judgement
见过	have seen
见好 (hǎo)	get better; on the mend

69

见后	see behind
见面	meet; see
见前	see in front
见上	see above
见下	see below

Radical: 辶　一　二　キ　井　井　讲　进

7 strokes

jìn

Meanings and examples

(1) advance; move forward: 前进 strive forward; move forward
(2) enter: 进小学 enter primary school; 进大学 enter university
(3) into; in: 车进来 the car comes in

进车里	enter a car; get into a car
进大学	enter university
进出	pass in and out; turnover
进出口	entrances and exits; exit; imports and exports
进发 (fā)	set out; start
进过	have entered
进见	call on (somebody holding high office); have an audience with
进进出出	coming in and going out
进口	import; entrance
进来	come in; enter; get in
进去	go in; get in; enter
进行 (xíng)	be in progress; carry on

经

jīng

Radical: 纟

8 strokes

L 纟 纟 纟 纪 纪 经 经 经

Meanings and examples

(1) through: 经过 go through
(2) endure: 经得起 can withstand; endure
(3) classic: 五经 the *Five Classics*

经不起	can't withstand; can't bear with
经得(de)起	withstand; bear; endure
经过	pass; go through; undergo
经心	careful; mindful; conscientious
经学	study of Confucian classics

就

jiù

Radical: 亠

12 strokes

丶 二 六 六 亠 亨 京 京 京 就 就 就

Meanings and examples

(1) at once: 我这就去。 I'll go at once.
(2) only: 就这一只，没有了。 This is the only one left. There's no more.
(3) even if: 你就不说，我也会知道。 Even if you don't tell me, I'll know it anyway.

就地 (dì)	on the spot
就可以…	can...
就去	go right away

就来了	coming
就是	quite right; exactly; precisely; even if
就是说	that is to say; in other words; namely
就学	go to school
就要	be about to; be going to; be on the point of
就要这只	this is the one wanted
就以为…	so think that…
就会用到/上了	it'll be used
就在这里	right here

Radical: 廾   ⁻ 二 于 开

4 strokes

kāi

Meanings and examples

(1) open; open up: 开个口 make a hole; 开口 open one's mouth
(2) start; operate: 开工 start work; 开动 start (machine)

开车	drive or start a car/train
开道	clear the way
开动	start; set in motion; move
开发 (fā)	develop; open up; exploit
开工	go into operation; start
开国	found a state or nation
开过	already opened
开会	hold or attend a meeting
开口	open one's mouth; start to talk
开口子	break; burst

开来看看　open and see
开明　　　enlightened
开头　　　begin; start
开心　　　happy; rejoice
开学　　　school opens

Radical: 目　一 二 三 手 手 看看看看

9 strokes

kān; kàn

Meanings and examples

(1) look after: 看 (kān) 家 look after the house
(2) visit: 我去看 (kàn) 他。 I'll go and see him.
(3) read: 看 (kàn) 不了 can't read through

看(kān)车　　　　　look after the vehicle
看(kān)家　　　　　look after the house
看不出　　　　　　can't make out; can't tell
看不到　　　　　　can't see
看不了 (liǎo)　　　can't read through; can't see all
看不起　　　　　　look down upon
看成　　　　　　　regard as
看出　　　　　　　make out; see
看到　　　　　　　see; catch sight of
看得 (de) 起　　　think highly of
看多了 (le)　　　have seen something often enough
看过　　　　　　　seen; read
看好(hǎo)了 (le)　have seen; have read

73

看看	have a look
看见	see; catch sight of
看来	it seems/appears; it looks as if
看来看去	look here and there; look around
看起来	it seems/appears; it looks as if
看上	take a fancy to
看上不看下	snobbish
看头	something worth seeing or reading
看样子	it seems/appears; it looks as if; looking at the situation
看一看	have a look
看中 (zhòng)	take a fancy to
看做	look upon as; regard as

Radical: 一 ⟨一 亅 亠 冂 口 可⟩

5 strokes

kě

Meanings and examples

(1) can (modal): 可以做 can do
(2) fit; suit: 可口 tasty

可不是	Isn't it so?
可见	it is thus clear that; visible
可可	cocoa
可口	good to eat; tasty
可人	one who has strengths worth extrolling; satisfying

74

可是	but; yet; however
可心	satisfying
可行 (xíng)	feasible
可以	can; may
可以吃	able to eat
可以看	able to see
可以上去	can go up
可以用	able to use
可以走了	can leave
可要小心	should be careful

Radical: 口 丨 冂 口

3 strokes

kǒu

Meanings and examples

(1) mouth: 我的口 my mouth
(2) opening; entrance: 进出口 entrance and exit
(3) classifier: 三口人 three people
(4) cut; hole: 一个口子 a hole

口吃	stutter; stammer
口头	oral
口头上	orally; verbally
口子	opening; hole; cut; tear

来
lái

Radical: 一 | 一 一 一 一 二 平 未 来

7 strokes

Meanings and examples

(1) come; arrive: 我从中国来。 I come from China.
(2) ever since: 从来 all along
(3) future; coming; next: 来年 the coming year

来不得 (de)	won't do
来到	arrive; come
来得 (de)	competent; equal to
来回	make a round trip; go to a place and come back
来回来去	back and forth; over and over again
来来去去	back and forth
来年	the coming year; next year
来人	bearer; messenger
来头	connections; backing

老
lǎo

Radical: 耂 | 一 十 土 尹 耂 老

6 strokes

Meanings and examples

(1) old; aged: 老人 old man or woman
(2) very: 老行 (háng) 家 very experienced person of the trade
(3) always: 老想 always think
(4) native; old place: 老家 native place/old home

老成	experienced; steady
老大	old; eldest child; the chief of a group
老道人	old Taoist priest
老二	the second child or brother
老工人	old workman/worker
老过他	older than him
老行 (háng) 家	expert or very experienced person of the trade
老好 (hǎo) 人	one who tries never to offend anybody
老几	order of seniority among brothers or sisters
老家	native place; old home
老了 (le)	getting old
老没见他	have not seen him for a long time
老年	old age
老人	old man or woman; the aged
老人家	a respectful form of address for an old person
老少 (shāo)	young and old
老天	God; Heavens
老头	old man; old chap
老头子	old fogey; old codger; old man
老小	grown-ups and children; one's family
老子	Lao Zi, an ancient Chinese philosopher
老子 (zi)	father

Radical: ⁷ 「⁷ 了」

2 strokes

了

le; liǎo

Meanings and examples

(1) know clearly; understand: 明了 (liǎo) understand
(2) end; finish: 了 (liǎo) 事 get something over; 吃了 (le) ate

了不得 (de)	terrific; extraordinary; terrible; awful
了不起	amazing; terrific; extraordinary
了得 (de)	to exclaim that the situation is grave
了了	know clearly
了事	dispose of a matter; get something over

* 了 pronounced *le* when it's used after the verb or adjective.

Radical: 里 「丨 口 曰 日 甲 甲 里 里」

7 strokes

里

lǐ

Meanings and examples

(1) lining; inside: 里面 inside
(2) to indicate the place or location: 这里 here; 那里 there
(3) a Chinese unit of length (about ½ km): 三里 three *li*

里面	inside; interior
里头	inside; interior
里子	lining

么

me

Radical: 厶 丿 厶 么

3 strokes

Meanings and examples

(1) used as a suffix to complement the question word: 什么
what; 怎么 why
(2) used to complement the exclamation word: 多么 how; 这么
such; so

没

méi; mò

Radical: 氵 丶 冫 氵 沪 沪 沙 没

7 strokes

Meanings and examples

(1) not have; there's not: 没 (méi) 人 there's no one
(2) not so: 没 (méi) 那么好 not as good as
(3) disappear; hide: 出没 (mò) to appear and disappear

没得 (de) 说 的 (de)	really good; there's no need to say any more about it
没大没小	impolite (to an elder)
没回家	haven't returned home
没看见	didn't see
没见过	never seen
没来	haven't come
没去过	never been to (somewhere)
没人	there's no one
没什么	it doesn't matter/there's nothing

没事	have nothing to do; it's no matter
没说	didn't say
没想到	didn't think of/expect
没想过	never thought of
没心	heartless
没学过	never learnt
没用	useless
没有	not have; there's not

Radical: 亻 ㇒ 亻 亻 仟 们

5 strokes

men

Meaning and example

(1) a suffix for the plural form of personal nouns and pronouns:
你们 you; 人们 people; 他们 they; 我们 we

Radical: 面 一 ㇒ 丆 币 而 而 面 面

9 strokes

miàn

Meanings and examples

(1) face: 面子 face
(2) side; surface; cover: 四面 four sides
(3) noodles; flour: 吃面 eat noodles

| 面对 | confront; face |
| 面对面 | face to face; facing each other |

80

面发 (fā) 起来	the dough has risen
面前	in (the) face of; in front of
面人	dough figurine
面子	face; reputation; image

Radical: 日   丨 冂 冃 日 旳 明 明 明

8 strokes

míng

Meanings and examples

(1) bright: 天明了 (le) day is breaking
(2) clear: 不明 not clear
(3) immediately following in time: 明年 next year

明后天	tomorrow or the day after tomorrow
明了 (liǎo)	understand; be clear about
明明	obviously; undoubtedly
明年	next year
明天	tomorrow; the near future
明知	know perfectly well; be fully aware

Radical: 阝   ⁊ ヨ ヨ 月 那 那

6 strokes

nà

Meaning and example

(1) that: 那是我的。 That's mine.

那个	that
那个小子	that fellow
那会	at that time; then
那里	there; that place
那么	like that; in that way; about; so
那么点	so little; so few
那么说	in that case; from what's said
那么样	so; such; like that
那时	at that time; then; in those days
那时候	at that time; in those days
那是	that is
那样	like that; of that kind; such (a thing); such as that; so

Radical: 亻   ノ 亻 亻 亻 你 你 你

7 strokes

nǐ

Meaning and example

(1) you (pronoun): 你看 you look; take a look

你不对	You're wrong.
你吃	you eat
你打人	You've beaten someone.
你大过我	You're older/more senior than I.
你的车	your car
你的家	your house/family
你的事	your problem or affair

你好	How are you?
你会	you know; you can
你看	you look
你看看	You have a look.
你可以…	you can…
你老了 (le)	You're getting old.
你们	you (plural)
你行 (xíng)	You're capable.
你走吧	You'd better go.

年
nián

Radical: ⺊ | ⺊ ⺊ ⺊ ⺊ ⺌ 年

6 strokes

Meanings and examples

(1) year: 去年 last year
(2) age: 年过八十 above eighty years old
(3) New Year: 过年 celebrate or spend the New Year

年成	the year's harvest
年成不好	a lean year
年会	annual meeting
年来	this year; these years
年年	every year; year after year
年少 (shào)	young
年时 (shí)	year; times
年头	year; times; harvest

| 年下 | the first half month of the Chinese calendar year |
| 年中 | mid-year |

Radical: 走　一　十　土　丰　走　走　起　起　起

10 strokes

qǐ

Meanings and examples

(1) rise; get up: 起来 get up
(2) start: 从明天起 starting from tomorrow
(3) batch; group: 分三起出发 set out in three groups
(4) together 一起

起点	starting point
起动	start; switch on (a machine)
起家	grow and thrive; build up
起见	for the purpose of; in order to
起开	step aside; stand aside
起来	get up; sit up; rise to one's feet
起事	start an armed struggle; rise in rebellion
起头	start; originate
起行 (xíng)	set out
起用	reinstate (an official who has retired or been dismissed)
起子 (zi)	bottle opener; screwdriver

前	Radical: 丷 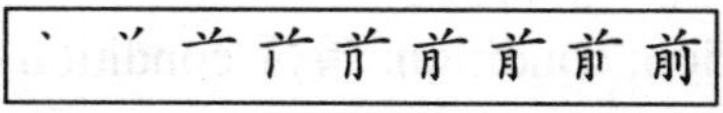 9 strokes

qián

Meanings and examples

(1) front 前面
(2) go forward 前进
(3) former; first: 前六天 the first six days

前后	from beginning to end; in front and behind
前后六天	about six days
前进	advance; go forward
前看后看	look before and after; look at the front and back
前面	in front; ahead; above
前年	the year before last
前前后后	the whole story; the ins and outs
前人	forefathers; predecessors
前事	past experience
前天	the day before yesterday
前头	in front; ahead

情	Radical: 忄 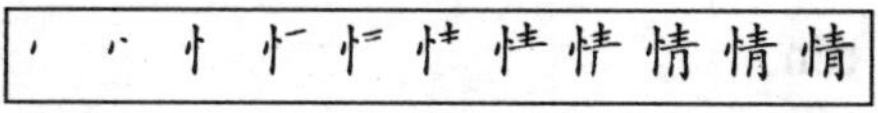 11 strokes

qíng

Meanings and examples

(1) feeling; affection; sentiment: 情分 (fen) mutual affection
(2) favour: 说情 plead for mercy on behalf of somebody

(3) situation; condition: 国情 condition of a country

情分 (fen)   mutual affection
情面   feelings; sensibilities
情人   sweetheart; lover

Radical: 土   一 十 土 去 去
5 strokes

qù

Meanings and examples

(1) go; leave: 出去 go out
(2) of last year: 去年 last year

去过   have been to
去年   last year

Radical: 人   丿 人
2 strokes

rén

Meanings and examples

(1) man; person: 人们 people
(2) a person engaged in certain type of job: 工人 worker
(3) everyone 人人
(4) personality; character: 为人 conduct oneself

人大   the National People's Congress

86

人道	humanity; human
人工	man-made; artificial; man-day; manpower
人和	support of the people
人家	household; family; other person or people; I
人口	population; number of people
人们	people; men; the public
人面	face
人情	human feelings; human relationship; favour; gift
人人	everyone
人上人	outstanding person
人事	human affairs; personnel matters
人头	the number of people; relations with people
人为	artificial; man-made
人心	popular feeling; the will of the people
人行 (xíng) 道	pavement; sidewalk
人中	philtrum

Radical: 卜 | 丨 卜 上

3 strokes

shàng

Meanings and examples

(1) up; upper; upward: 看上去 look up
(2) previous: 上一面 the previous page
(3) go up 上去
(4) go to: 上学 go to school
(5) at: 会上 at the meeting

上不来， 　下不去	can neither come up nor go down
上车	get on (a vehicle); embark
上工	go to work
上好 (hǎo)	best quality; first class
上回	last chapter; last time; previously
上家	the person on one's right (Chinese custom) when playing cards or drinkers' wager game
上进	go forward; make progress
上进心	the urge for improvement
上口	be able to read aloud fluently
上来	come up
上来看	come up and see
上面	above; over; on top of
上面说的	above-mentioned
上前	go forward
上去	go up
上上	the very best
上天	Heaven; fly sky-high; God
上头	above; over; on top of
上我家	go to my house
上下	high and low; from top to bottom; up and down
上行 (xíng)	up; upgoing
上学	go to school
上有老， 　下有小	referring to someone who has the old and the young to take care

少

Radical: 小 ⼁ ⼋ ⼩ 少

4 strokes

shǎo; shào

Meanings and examples

(1) few; little; less: 人少 (shǎo) 车多 few people but many cars
(2) short of; lack: 我们还少 (shǎo) 三个人。 We're still three men short.
(3) lose; be missing: 一个也不少 (shǎo) not even one is missing
(4) young: 老少 (shào) old and young
(5) son of rich family; young master: 三少 (shào) the third young master

少不得/少不了 (liǎo)	can't do without; can't dispense with
少不了你的	You'll not be left out.
少过	less than
少候	wait a moment
少见	rare
少看	seldom see
少时	after a while; a moment later
少说	talk less
少学	learn less
少有的	rare
少做	do less
少 (shào) 年	early youth; juvenile
少 (shào) 年老成	mature for one's age

Radical: 亻 丿 亻 什 什

4 strokes

shén

Meanings and examples

(1) to doubt: 什么 what; 什么人 who; 什么时候 when
(2) to indicate uncertain things or matters: 有什么就说什么。
Just say what's on one's mind; 想什么就说什么。 Just say
what one thinks.

什么   what
什么的   so on and so forth
什么人   Who is that?
什么时候   When is it?
什么事   What's the matter?

Radical: 日 丨 冂 冃 日 日- 时 时

7 strokes

shí

Meanings and examples

(1) time; times; days: 现时 now
(2) hour: 六小时 six hours
(3) often; frequently 时时

时分   time
时候   time
时时   often; constantly
时事   current events; current affairs

时下　　　　at present
时行 (xíng)　popular
时有出现　　occur now and then
时样　　　　the latest fashion

Radical: 是

9 strokes

丶　丆　日　日　旦　早　早　昮　是

shì

Meanings and examples

(1) correct; right: 你说得是。 What you said is right.
(2) yes; right: 是，我会的。 Yes, I will.
(3) verb to be: 我是人 I'm a person.

是不是　whether or not
是的　　yes; right; that's it

Radical: 一

8 strokes

一　丆　丙　币　百　写　耳　写　事

shì

Meanings and examples

(1) matter; affair; thing; business: 国事 national or state affairs
(2) trouble; accident: 出事 have an accident
(3) job: 有事做 have the job

事后　after the event; afterwards
事前　before the event; in advance

事情	affair; matter; thing; business
事事	everything
事在人为	It all depends on human effort.
事主	the victim of a crime

Radical: 讠

`丶 讠 讠 讱 讱 说 说 说 说`

9 strokes

shuō

Meanings and examples

(1) speak; talk; say: 你说得很对。 What you said is quite right.
(2) explain: 他说了又说，我还是不会。 He explained time and again but I still couldn't understand him.

说不得	unspeakable; not to be mentioned
说不过去	can't be justified or explained
说不来	can't get along; don't see eye to eye
说不上	can't say; can't tell; not worth mentioning
说到	speak of
说到做到	do what one says
说道	say
说得不好	not well said or spoken about
说得多	much is spoken about
说得过去	justifiable; can be said to be so
说得好	a good speech
说得来	can get along; be on good terms
说过	said; mentioned
说好	come to an agreement or understanding

说和	mediate; make a settlement
说来说去	regardless of what is said
说了	said
说明	explain; illustrate; show
说起来	talk about
说情	plead for mercy for somebody; intercede
说三道四	make irresponsible remarks
说什么	whatever is said; no matter how
说一不二	mean what one says, stand by one's word
说中 (zhòng)	say to the point; say correctly

Radical: 亻   ノ 亻 亻 仴 他

5 strokes

tā

Meanings and examples

(1) he (pronoun): 他走了。 He has gone.
(2) other: 他用 other uses; 已他去 has left

他不要	He doesn't want.
他回了	He has gone back.
他会 ...	He knows/can…
他家在 ...	His home is at…
他看不出 ...	He can't see/make out…
他可以	He can…
他来了	He has come.
他来不来	Will he come?
他们	they

他年	other years (in future)
他人	another person; others
他要…	He wants…
他想…	He thinks…
他走了	He has gone.

Radical: 天 一 二 チ 天

4 strokes

tiān

Meanings and examples

(1) sky; heaven 上天
(2) day: 三天 three days
(3) weather: 好天 fine weather
(4) God; heaven: 天知道 God knows

天车	overhead travelling crane; crown block
天大	extremely big
天大的好事	an excellent thing
天地	heaven and earth; world; field of activity; scope of operation
天分 (fēn)	special endowments; natural gift; talent
天国	Heaven; paradise
天候	weather
天明	daybreak; dawn
天年	natural span of life
天上	in the sky
天时	weather; climate; timeliness
天天	every day; daily

94

天下	land under heaven; the world rule; domination
天知道	God knows
天主	God
天子	the Son of Heaven — the emperor

Radical: 大 　 ` ` ㆒ 头 头

5 strokes

tóu

Meanings and examples

(1) head: 我的头 my head
(2) hair 头发
(3) top; end: 头上 on top of the head
(4) chief or head: 我们的头 our head
(5) first: 头三天 the first three days
(6) beginning or end: 从头 from the very beginning

头发 (fà)	hair
头里	in front; ahead; in advance
头面	ornaments for adorning women's hair and face
头年	last year; the previous year
头人	tribal chief; headman
头天	the day before; the previous day
头头	head; chief; leader
头头是道	clear and logical; closely reasoned and well argued
头子	chieftain; chief; boss

95

Radical: `

`　丿　力　为

4 strokes

wéi; wèi

Meanings and examples

(1) do; act: 事在人为 (wéi)。 Human effort is the decisive factor.
(2) be; mean: 一小时为 (wéi) 六十分。 An hour is made up of 60 minutes.
(3) for: 为 (wèi) 他做事 work for him
(4) why 为 (wèi) 什么

为 (wéi) 人	behave; conduct oneself
为 (wéi) 主	give first place to; give priority to
为大家	for all; for everyone
为国为家	for the nation and the family
为了 (le)	for; for the sake of; in order to
为人做事	work for someone
为什么	why
为他说情	intercede for him
为我	for me/us
为自己	for me

Radical: 戈 一 二 于 手 我 我 我

7 strokes

wǒ

Meanings and examples

(1) I 我 (pronoun)
(2) self 自我

我不要	I don't want.
我吃	I eat
我出去	I go out
我打他	I beat him
我的	my; mine
我国	my nation; my country
我还 (hái) 好	I'm still all right.
我和你	you and I
我很好	I'm very fine.
我回家	I go home.
我回去…	I return to…
我会做	I know how to do
我家	my house; my home
我见	my opinion; I see
我进去	I go in
我经过 …	I pass by…
我就 …	I'll then…
我开车	I drive
我看	I see; I think
我口	my mouth

我来了	Here, I come!
我老了	I'm old!
我没用	I'm useless.
我们	we
我们的	our; ours
我上去	I go up.
我是 …	I'm…
我说	I say
我为人人	I work/do for the people.
我下来	I come down.
我想	I think
我学	I learn
我要	I want
我要回家	I want to go home.
我有	I have
我用	I use
我在 …	I'm at…
我知道	I know
我自己来	I'll do it myself.
我走了	I make a move.

xià

Radical: 卜 一 丁 下
3 strokes

Meanings and examples

(1) below; down; under: 以下 below; the following

98

(2) lower; inferior: 上、中、下 the upper, the middle and the lower

(3) next; latter; second: 下个月 the next month

(4) get off; descend; alight: 下车 get off a car or bus

(5) put in: 下面 put in the noodles

(6) be less than: 不下 no less than

下不来	refuse to come down; can't be accomplished; feel embarrassed
下车	get off a car or bus
下地	go to the fields; leave a sickbed
下工	come or go off work; stop work
下家	next person (this term is only used in games)
下来	come down
下面	below; under; next; lower level
下情	conditions at the lower levels; feelings or wishes of the masses
下去	go down; descend; go on
下人	servant
下头	below; lower level
下行 (xíng)	down
下一年	the next year

Radical: 王

8 strokes

一 二 干 王 珒 珇 现 现

xiàn

Meanings and examples

(1) present; current; existing: 现时 now

99

(2) appear; show: 出现 emerge; appear

现成	ready-made
现吃现做	cook for immediate consumption
现出	show; appear
现地	on the spot; scene
现时	now; at present
现下	now; at present
现学现用	apply immediately after learning
现行 (xíng)	currently in effect; in force; in operation
现有	available now; existing
现在	now; at present; today

想

Radical: 心   一 十 才 木 相 相 相 相 相 相 想 想 想

13 strokes

xiǎng

Meanings and examples

(1) think: 想到 think of
(2) suppose: 我想他不会来了。 I don't think he'll come.
(3) want to: 我想去。 I want to go.
(4) miss: 我很想你。 I miss you.

想不到	unexpected
想不开	take things too hard; take a matter to heart
想不起	can't recall
想吃	want to eat
想出	think of (way)
想出点子	think of a way

想到	think of; call to mind
想得不对	didn't think right
想得到	think; expect; imagine
想得开	doesn't take to heart
想过	have already given thought to
想好	make up one's mind; well thought of
想好了 (le)	made up one's mind
想回家	want to go home
想家	homesick; miss the family
想见	infer; gather
想看	want to have a look
想来	presumably; suppose
想起	remember; recall
想事情	thinking of something
想说	want to say
想头	idea; hope
想想	think about
想学	want to learn
想要	want
想要说	want to say
想一想	think over
想用	want to use
想知道	want to know
想走	want to leave or make a move
想做	want to do

Radical: 小 | 亅 小 小

3 strokes

xiǎo

Meanings and examples

(1) small; little; petty; minor: 小国 small country
(2) young: 一家老小 the old and young; the whole family

小不点	very small; tiny; tiny tot
小车	small vehicle; wheelbarrow
小吃	snack; refreshments
小道	a small path; a small sidewalk
小个的	the small one
小个子	a little chap; a small fellow
小工	unskilled labourer
小过	a minor offence; a trivial offence
小看	look down upon; belittle
小看人	look down upon someone; belittle someone
小可	ordinary; the humble address to oneself
小口	small opening/mouth
小年	a Chinese calendar year in which the last month has 29 days
小人	a person of low position; a mean person
小时	hour; childhood
小时候	childhood
小事	trifle; petty thing
小说	novel; fiction
小说家	novelist

小天地	one's own little world
小头	small head
小心	take care; be careful
小我	individual
小学	primary school
小样	galley proof
小子 (zi)	boy; fellow; chap

Radical: 心　㇐ 心 心 心

4 strokes

xīn

Meanings and examples

(1) heart: 我的心 my heart
(2) mind; feeling; intention: 好心 good intention
(3) centre; core: 中心 centre

心不在	inattentive; absent-minded
心得 (dé)	what one has learned from work, study, etc.
心地 (dì)	a person's mind, character, moral nature, etc.
心动	one's mind is perturbed
心口	the pit of the stomach
心口不一	what one says is different from what one thinks
心里	in the heart; at heart; in (the) mind
心里有事	have something on one's mind
心情	frame (state) of mind; mood
心情不一样	feel differently
心上	at heart

心上人	sweetheart
心事	something weighing on one's mind; a load on one's mind; worry
心头	mind; heart
心想事成	accomplish what one thinks/plans
心中 (zhōng)	in the heart
心子	centre; core; heart

行

Radical: 彳   ノ ク イ 彳 彳 行

6 strokes

xíng; háng

Meanings and examples

(1) go; walk: 行 (xíng) 走 walk
(2) can; all right: 不行 (xíng) won't do
(3) do: 可行 (xíng) feasible
(4) line; row: 三行 (háng) three lines or three rows
(5) seniority among brothers and sisters: 我行 (háng) 二，你行几？ I'm the second among my siblings, what about you?
(6) trade; line of business: 我做这一行。 I'm in this line of business.

行道*	trade; profession
行会*	guild
行家*	expert; connoisseur
行情*	quotations (on the market); prices
行车	drive a vehicle
行动	move about; act; action; operation
行好	act charitably; be merciful

行进	march forward; advance
行经	go by; menstruate
行了 (le)	all right; O.K.
行人	pedestrian
行人道	sidewalk; footpath
行时	(of a thing) be in vogue; be all the rage
行事	act; handle matters
行头	actor's costumes and paraphernalia
行为	action; behaviour; conduct
行走	walk

* 行 pronounced *háng*

学
8 strokes

xué

Radical: 子 　 丶 丶 丷 ⺍ 兴 学 学 学

Meanings and examples

(1) study; learn: 学会 learn; master
(2) imitate: 学他开车的样子 imitate his way of driving
(3) school; college: 小学 primary school; 中学 secondary school; 大学 university

学到	master
学到老	learn as long as one lives
学分	credit
学过	has learnt
学好	learn from good examples
学会	learn; master; society

105

学年	academic year; school year
学前	preschool
学时	class hour; period
学说	theory; doctrine
学子	students
学走	learn how to walk

Radical: 木   一 十 才 木 木 术 栏 栏 样 样 样

10 strokes

yàng

Meanings and examples

(1) appearance; shape 样子
(2) sample; model; pattern: 打样 draw a design
(3) kind; type: 几样 a few types

样样	each and every; every kind; all
样样都会	know how to do every kind
样子	shape; appearance; manner; sample

Radical: 女   一 一 一 两 两 西 要 要 要

9 strokes

yào

Meanings and examples

(1) important; essential: 要事 important matter
(2) want; ask for; wish: 我要出去。 I want to go out.
(3) must; should: 要好 (hǎo) 好 (hāo) 学 must learn hard

106

(4) shall; will; be going to: 要到了 about to reach
(5) if; suppose; in case: 要是你不回来，我就不走。 If you don't come back, I won't leave.

要不	otherwise; or else; or
要不得 (dé)	no good; intolerable
要不是	if it were not for; but for
要不要	want or not
要不要去*	whether to go or not
要道	thoroughfare
要得 (dé)	good; fine
要地 (dì)	important place; strategic point
要点	main points; essentials; the gist
要好 (hǎo)	be on good terms; be close friends
要回	ask (somebody) to return
要来了 (le)	coming
要么	or; either… or …
要面子	be keen on face-saving; be anxious to keep up appearances
要去	want to go
要人	very important person (V.I.P.)
要是	if; suppose; in case
要事	important matter
要用	want to use
要走	about to leave

* can be used interchangeably with other verbs

Radical: 乛 | 乛 乜 也

3 strokes

yě

Meaning and example

(1) also; too; as well; either: 你不走，我也不走。 If you're not leaving, neither will I.

也不成	neither successful nor completed
也不吃	also don't feel like eating
也不动	also don't want to move
也不多	not many too; not much too
也不好	also not good
也不回来	also don't come back
也不会	also don't know
也不来	don't come
也不去	don't go
也不是	neither…nor
也不说	neither say
也不想	neither think
也不行	neither work
也不要	neither want
也不用	neither use
也不在那里	neither be there
也不知	neither know
也不走	neither go
也不做工	neither work (do a job)
也成	also accepted

108

也对	also correct; also true; also right
也好	may as well
也会	know too
也可以	feasible too
也来	also come
也是	right; true; correct
也说	say too
也想	want too
也要	want too
也行 (xíng)	feasible too
也有	also have; there's also
也用	use it too
也只好	have to; can't help but

Radical: 已 ㄱ ㄱ 已

3 strokes

yǐ

Meanings and examples

(1) stop; cease; end: 不已 endlessly
(2) already 已经

| 已经 | already |
| 已知 | already known |

Radical: 人 | ✓ ✓ 以 以

4 strokes

以

yǐ

Meanings and examples

(1) use; take: 以我之见 in my opinion
(2) to show the limit or the range: 以上 above; 三年以前 three years ago
(3) according to; because of: 以学分来看 judge according to the credits

以对	to respond; to deal with
以后	after; afterwards; later; hereafter
以我之见	in my opinion
以我为主	take myself as the key factor
以来	since
以前	before; formerly; previously
以上	more than; over; above; the above; the above-mentioned
以为	think; believe; consider
以下	below; under; the following

Radical: 几 | 丿 几 月 月 用

5 strokes

用

yòng

Meanings and examples

(1) use; employ; apply: 用人 employ a person
(2) expenses: 家用 family expenses

(3) usefulness; use: 没用 useless
(4) need: 不用 no need

用不了 (liǎo)	have more than is needed; less than
用车	use the car
用过	used
用人	employ a person; servant
用事	act; be in power
用心	diligently; attentively; motive; intention
用以	in order to: so as to

Radical: 广 一 广 广 有 有 有

6 strokes

yǒu

Meanings and examples

(1) have; possess: 我有一个心。 I have a heart.
(2) there's; exist: 家里有人。 There's someone at home.
(3) some: 有人说。 Some say.

有成	achievement
有车	in possession of a car
有道是	so as said
有的	some
有的是	have plenty of; there's no lack of
有点	some; a little
有会子	quite a long while; quite some time
有了	already have; here it's
有年	for years

有情	affection
有情人	lover
有人	there's someone
有人说	some say
有时	sometimes; at times; now and then
有事	something happens; some matter that needs to be attended to
有头有面	prestigious; reputable
有为	promising
有我在	I'm present; in my presence
有心	have a mind to; set one's mind on; purposely
有心人	a person who sets his mind on doing something useful; an observant and conscientious person
有一天	one day
有用	useful
有样学样	follow one's example

又

yòu

Radical: 又 ﾌ 又

2 strokes

Meanings and examples

(1) again; repeating: 一年又一年 year after year
(2) alternately: 又要又不要 can't make up the mind whether want or not
(3) and: 二又四分之一 two and a quarter

| 又不 | not again |
| 又多又好 | both many and good |

112

又到	come/arrive again
又好看又好吃	both attractive and palatable
又见面	meet again
又回来	return again
又来了	come or happen again
又是他	It's him again
又想	reconsider
又要	want again
又要面对	confront again

Radical: 广 一 ナ ナ 存 存 在

6 strokes

zài

Meanings and examples

(1) exist; be living: 人还在 he's living
(2) in (time, place): 在去年 during last year; 在家 at home
(3) rest with; depend on: 事在人为。 It all depends on human effort.

在行 (háng)	be knowledgeable in something; specialize in a field
在会上	at the meeting
在家	at home
在家人	layman
在去年	during last year
在上的	the superior
在下	"I" (humble self address)
在下的	the subordinate

在心里/中 (zhōng)	feel concerned; mind
在在	everywhere; in all respects
在这里	here; at this place
在中国	in China

Radical: 心 ノ ⺊ ⺊ ⺊ ⺁ ⺁ 怎 怎 怎

9 strokes

zěn

Meaning and example

(1) why; how: 你怎不开口？ Why don't you speak up?

怎的	why; how; what
怎么	why; how; what
怎么得了	where will it all end; how terrible it would be
怎么吃	how to eat
怎么不对	what's wrong
怎么分	how to divide/share among…
怎么看	how to see
怎么去	how to go there
怎么说	what to say
怎么行 (xíng)	how can it be
怎么样	how
怎样	how

这

Radical: 辶

` 亠 亠 文 文 讠 这 这

7 strokes

zhè; zhèi

Meanings and examples

(1) this: 这 (zhè) 个国家 this country; 这 (zhèi) 三天 these three days

(2) now: 他这 (zhè) 才知道我是好人。 Only now does he know I'm a good person; 我这就走。 I'm leaving right now.

这都是	all because of this
这个	this one; so; such
这个人	this person
这会	now; at the moment
这回	this time
这就不对了	This is wrong.
这就对了	That's right.
这就来了	Come right away!
这里	here
这么	so; such; this way; like this
这么点	just this bit
这么说	in this case
这么样	so; like this
这是	this is
这下子	this time
这样	so; such; like this; this way

Radical: 矢　丿　㇏　㇑　㇒　矢　矢　知　知

8 strokes

zhī

Meanings and examples

(1) know; realize; be aware of 知道
(2) knowledge: 知行 (xíng) knowing and doing

知道	know; realize; be aware of
知己	intimate; understanding; bosom friend
知了 (liǎo)	cicada
知情	know the facts of a case or the details of an incident
知情人	person in the know; an insider
知人	know one's ability
知人知面不知心	know a person's face but not his heart; know a person for a long time without understanding his true nature
知人之明	ability to appreciate a person's character and capability; having a keen insight into a person's character
知心	intimate; understanding
知行	knowing and doing

Radical: 、 丶 ㇋ 之

3 strokes

之
zhī

Meanings and examples

(1) (pronoun): 为之 do something
(2) of: 老人之家 old folks' home

之后   later; after; afterwards
之前   before; prior to; ago

Radical: 口 丨 冂 口 尸 只

5 strokes

只
zhī; zhǐ

Meanings and examples

(1) only; merely: 家里只 (zhǐ) 有一个人。 There is only one
    person at home.
(2) classifier for animals and boats: 十只 (zhī) ten (animals/
    boats)

只不过   only; just; merely
只得 (dē)   have no alternative but to do something
只好   have to; be forced to do something
只发现   discover (one thing or person) only
只见   see (one thing or person) only
只看   look at (one thing or person) only
只是   merely; only; just
只说不做   to talk only and take no action

只要   as long as; provided that
只有   only; alone
只用   use (something) only

 Radical: 丨   丶 口 口 中

4 strokes

zhōng; zhòng

Meanings and examples

(1) centre; middle: 中 (zhōng) 心 centre, heart
(2) in; among: 心中 (zhōng) in the heart
(3) middle; mid: 中 (zhōng) 年 middle age
(4) sit for; good for: 不中 (zhōng) 用 good for nothing
(5) China: 可为中(zhōng) 用 things that are of use to China
(6) hit; fit exactly: 说中 (zhòng) hit the nail upon the head; say to the point

中吃	tasty
中点	midpoint
中国	China
中国人	Chinese
中和	neutralization
中看	pleasant to the eye
中看不中吃	looks nice but does not taste nice
中年	middle age
中年人	middle-aged person
中人	middleman; mediator
中天	culmination; meridian passage
中心	centre; heart; core; hub

中心点	centre
中学	high school; secondary school; Chinese learning
中用	of use; useful
中子	neutron
中(zhòng)的(dì)	hit the mark

Radical: 王　`　一　二　㣺　主

5 strokes

zhǔ

Meanings and examples

(1) host; master: 主人 master
(2) owner: 车主 the owner of a car
(3) main; primary: 主要 main; important
(4) advocate: 主和 advocate peace

主从	principal and subordinate
主动	initiative
主和	advocate peace
主见	ideas or thoughts of one's own; one's own judgement
主人	host; master
主事	the person in charge
主要	main; chief; principal; major
主子	master; boss

Radical: 子　[⁷ 了 子]

3 strokes

zǐ; zi

Meanings and examples

(1) son; child: 三个小子 three boys；天子 the Son of Heaven — the emperor

(2) something small and hard: 一个子 a small piece or a copper coin

子时　　the period of the day from 11:00 p.m. to 1:00 a.m.

Radical: 自　[′ 亻 冂 白 自 自]

6 strokes

zì

Meanings and examples

(1) self; one's own: 自学 self-study

(2) from; since 自从

自成一家	(in calligraphy, painting, sculpture etc.) have a style of one's own; be unique in one's style
自从	since
自大	self-important; arrogant
自得	contented; self-satisfied; pleased with oneself; self-complacent
自动	voluntarily; automatic
自发	spontaneous

120

自己	oneself; one's own
自己人	people on one's own side; one of us
自己做	do something on one's own
自家	oneself
自来	from the beginning; in the first place; originally
自明	self-evident; self-explanatory; obvious
自是	naturally; of course
自我	self; oneself
自行 (xíng)	by oneself
自行(xíng)到来	voluntarily; of one's own accord
自行(xíng)车	bicycle
自学	study on one's own; self-study
自以为是	consider oneself (always) in the right
自用	obstinately holding to one's own views; opinionated; self-willed
自在	free; unrestrained; comfortable; at ease
自知之明	self-knowledge; self-awareness; self-consciousness
自主	act on one's own; decide for oneself

Radical: 走   ┌ 一 十 土 卡 キ 走 走 ┐

7 strokes

zǒu

Meanings and examples

(1) walk; go: 走动 walk about
(2) move: 打了就走 hit and run
(3) leave; go away: 走开 go away; get lost

121

走出去	walk out
走道	pavement; sidewalk; path
走的样子	the way one walks
走动	walk about; visit each other
走过	walk past
走回家	walk home
走回头	turn back
走开	go away
走来	come up to
走了	left
走起来	walk on; walk as if
走样	lose shape; go out of form

Radical: 亻

丿 亻 亻 仁 仁 佧 佧 佬 佬 做 做

11 strokes

zuò

Meanings and examples

(1) make; produce; manufacture: 这是他做的。 This was made by him.
(2) do; act; engage in: 做好事 do a good deed
(3) be; become: 做个好人 be a good person

做不到	unable to do or accomplish something
做不好	can't do something well
做不来	unable to do or accomplish something
做得到	accomplish; achieve; can do
做得多	do a lot

做得来	able to do or accomplish something
做得少	do a little
做个好人	be a good person
做工	do work; work
做过	have done something before
做好人	be a good person
做好事	do a good deed
做起	start doing
做人	conduct oneself; behave
做事	handle affairs; do something
做主	decide; take the responsibility for a decision; back up; support
做主人	be the host or master

11. Antonyms

1. 大 / 小　大车 / 小车　大国 / 小国　大事 / 小事
   大学 / 小学　大个子 / 小个子
   big/small　big car/smaller car　big nation/small nation
   major matter/minor matter　university/primary school
   a tall person/a little chap

2. 上 / 下　天上 / 地下　以上 / 以下　走上 / 走下
   上来 / 下来　上去 / 下去　上面 / 下面　上头 / 下头
   up/down　in the sky/on the ground　above/below
   walk up/walk down　come up/come down　go up/go down
   above/below　above/below

3. 前 / 后　以前 / 以后　人前 / 人后　前面 / 后面
   前年 / 后年　前头 / 后头
   front/rear　before/in future　in front of people/behind of people　the
   face/the back　last year/the year after next year　front/rear

4. 天 / 地　天上 / 地下　上天 / 下地
   heaven/earth　in the sky/on the ground
   ascend to heaven/descend to earth

5. 多 / 少　人多 / 人少　多一点 / 少一点　过多 / 过少
   abundant/little　many people/few people
   a little more/a little less　too much/too little

6. 老 / 少　老年人 / 少年人　老的 / 少的　老年 / 少年
   old/young　old person/youth　the old/the young　old age/ado-
   lescence

7. 来 / 去　来了 / 去了　进来 / 进去　出来 / 出去
   来年 / 去年　回来 / 回去
   come/go　arrived/gone　come in here/go in there
   come out here/go out　coming year/last year
   come back/go back

8. 进 / 出　进口 / 出口　进来 / 出来　进去 / 出去
   enter/exit　entrance or import/exit or export
   come in/come out　go in/go out

9. 你 / 我　你的 / 我的　你们 / 我们　你们的 / 我们的
   you/me　yours/mine　you/we　yours/ours

10. 这 / 那　这里 / 那里　这头 / 那头　这面 / 那面
    这回 / 那回　这人 / 那人　这家 / 那家　这天 / 那天
    这回事 / 那回事　这时 / 那时　这时候 / 那时候
    这里面 / 那里面　这个 / 那个　这里头 / 那里头
    this/that　here/there　this way/that way　this side/that side
    this time/that time　this man/that man
    this home/that home　this day/that day
    this matter/that matter　this moment/that moment
    this time/that time　in here/in there　this one/that one
    in here/in there

*   不大不小；不上不下；不前不后；不多不少
    neither too big nor too small; neither up nor down; neither
    front nor rear; neither too much nor too little

125

12. Interrogatives

1.	多不多？	Are there many (things)?/Is there too much?
2.	少不少？	Are there a few?/Is there too little?
3.	大不大？	Is it big?
4.	小不小？	Is it small?
5.	好不好？	Is it good?
6.	成不成？	Is it successful/feasible?
7.	动不动？	Is it moveable?
8.	对不对？	Is it right?
9.	会不会？	Is he able to?
10.	开不开？	Does he want to open it?
11.	见不见？	Does he want to meet him?
12.	看不看？	Does he want to see it?
13.	老不老？	Is he old?
14.	来不来？	Is he coming?
15.	去不去？	Is he going?
16.	是不是？	Is it so?
17.	上不上？	Is it going up?
18.	下不下？	Is it going down?
19.	学不学？	Does he want to learn?
20.	做不做？	Is he going to do it?
21.	要不要？	Does he want it?
22.	说不说？	Is he going to say it?
23.	走不走？	Is he leaving?
24.	回不回？	Is he returning?
25.	想不想？	Is he thinking of it?
26.	进不进？	Is he going in?
27.	用不用？	Does he use it?
28.	中(zhòng)不中？	Can he get it?/Can he think of it?
29.	和不和？	Are they going to draw?
30.	在不在？	Is he in?
31.	吃不吃？	Does he want to eat?

32.	可以不可以？	Can he?
33.	对口不对口？	Does it fit?
34.	对头不对头？	Is it all right?
35.	有用没有用？	Is it useful?
36.	看见不看见？	Is it visible?/Can he see it?
37.	回去不回去？	Is he going back?
38.	回家不回家？	Is he going home?
39.	回来不回来？	Is he coming back?
40.	进去不进去？	Is he going in?
41.	进来不进来？	Is he coming in?
42.	进口不进口？	Is he importing it?
43.	出口不出口？	Is he exporting it?
44.	出去不出去？	Is he going out?
45.	出来不出来？	Is he coming out?
46.	用心不用心？	Is he attentive?
47.	小心不小心？	Is he careful?
48.	打人不打人？	Is he beating someone?
49.	成事不成事？	Is it going to be accomplished?
50.	开车不开车？	Is he driving the car?
51.	开会不开会？	Is he holding a meeting?
52.	开工不开工？	Is he starting work?
53.	开动不开动？	Is he starting the machine?
54.	开学不开学？	Is the school open?
55.	开发不开发？	Is it developing?
56.	经过不经过？	Does he pass by…?
57.	知道不知道？	Does he know?
58.	分工不分工？	Is the work to be divided?
59.	过来不过来？	Is he coming?
60.	过去不过去？	Is he going there?
61.	在家不在家？	Is he at home?
62.	会做不会做？	Can he do it?
63.	会用不会用？	Can he use it?
64.	要走不要走？	Is he leaving?
65.	要说不要说？	Is he going to say it?

66.	要吃不要吃？	Does he want to eat?
67.	起来不起来？	Is he getting up?
68.	可吃不可吃？	Can he eat it?/Is it edible?
69.	可看不可看？	Can he see it?
70.	可用不可用？	Is it usable?
71.	中看不中看？	Is the appearance presentable?
72.	中用不中用？	Is he capable?
73.	出车不出车？	Is he driving?
74.	出国不出国？	Is he going abroad?
75.	出工不出工？	Is he going to work?
76.	分发不分发？	Is it distributed?
77.	道地不道地/ 地道不地道？	Is it real?
78.	自动不自动？	Is it automatic?
79.	自主不自主？	Can he make his own decision?
80.	主动不主动？	Is he taking the initiative?
81.	有心没有心？	Is he concerned?

* There are no pronouns in the Chinese text. To help learners understand the English translation, we add pronouns to complete the sentences.

13. Positives and Negatives

1.	看得见/看不见	can see/can't see
2.	看得成/看不成	be able to see (a show)/unable to see (a show)
3.	看得起/看不起	look up to/look down on
4.	看得了/看不了	be able to finish (reading or reviewing)/unable to finish (reading or reviewing)
5.	看得过/看不过	can tolerate/can't tolerate
6.	看得到/看不到	can see/can't see
7.	做得来/做不来	can do/can't do
8.	做得好/做不好	can do well/can't do well
9.	做得到/做不到	can accomplish/can't accomplish
10.	出得来/出不来	can go out/can't go out
11.	进得去/进不去	can enter/can't enter
12.	开得成/开不成	can set up/can't set up
13.	打得开/打不开	can open/can't open
14.	开得动/开不动	can start (the engine)/can't start (the engine)
15.	开得了工/开不了工	can start working/can't start working
16.	开得成学/开不成学	can start school/can't start school
17.	过得了/过不了	can survive/can't survive
18.	过得去/过不去	passable/not passable
19.	想得出/想不出	can think it out/can't think it out
20.	说得明/说不明	can explain it clearly/can't explain it clearly
21.	来得成/来不成	can come/can't come
22.	来得了/来不了	can come/can't come
23.	用得了/用不了	can be used/can't be used
24.	用得上/用不上	can be of use/can't be of use
25.	回得去/回不去	can return/can't return
26.	动得了/动不了	can move/can't move
27.	说得出/说不出	can speak out/can't speak out

28.	想得起/想不起	can recollect/can't recollect
29.	学得成/学不成	can master it/can't master it
30.	学得好/学不好	can learn well/can't learn well
31.	起得成/起不成	can get up/can't get up
32.	上得去/上不去	can mount/can't mount
33.	下得来/下不来	can come down/can't come down
34.	要得成/要不成	can have/can't have
35.	成得了事/成不了事	can accomplish it/can't accomplish it
36.	对头/不对头	something is right/something isn't right
37.	对口/不对口	fit one's taste/doesn't fit one's taste
38.	发动/不发动	launch/doesn't launch
39.	开动/不开动	start (the engine)/doesn't start (the engine)
40.	见得到/见不到	can see/can't see

14. "来……去也……不" Sentences

1. 看来看去也看不见。
   No matter how hard you try, you still can't see it.

2. 用来用去也用不了。
   No matter how much you spend, you still can't spend it all.

3. 想来想去也想不出。
   No matter how hard you think, you still can't think of an answer.

4. 走来走去也走不到。
   No matter how long you walk, you still can't reach the destination.

5. 开来开去也开不动。
   No matter how hard you try, you still can't start it.

6. 打来打去也打不开。
   No matter how hard you try, you still can't open it.

7. 说来说去也说不明。
   No matter how much you say, you still can't clarify it.

8. 做来做去也做不好。
   No matter how hard you try, you still can't do it well.

9. 学来学去也学不会。
   No matter how hard you study, you still can't understand it.

10. 吃来吃去也吃不了。
    No matter how much you eat, you still can't eat it up.

15. Common Expressions

不到	less than; not yet; under
不过	however; only; merely; yet; but
不是…就是…	either…or…
不只 …还	not only…but also
从…起	from (a particular time) onward
从…说起	begin FV+ing from
从…来	come from
从…去	from…to
从来没有	has/have never
从来不	never
对…	for…; to…; as for the…; regarding…
…多了	more than; over; much more
就是	right there is
就是这么来的	this is how it happened
可…的	…able; worth FV+ing
那还用说	needless to say
没有…就没有…	without … there would be no …
（前十数十量）	(past; last; before; ago) + (number) + (classifier)
前一天 / 前三年	the day before/over the first three years
为了…起见	for the sake of; in order to; because of
为了	in order to; for; for the purpose of
…就	… all right
和…一样	is the same as
以上 / 以下	above; more than / under; less than
左…上/在…下/ 在…中	on; at / on; at / in the middle of
以前/以后	before / later (since then)
一个又一个	one after another
一天又一天	one day after another
一年又一年	year after year

一个个 / 一天天/ 一年年	one by one / day by day / year by year
一…就	as soon as
这不 / 这不是	isn't it / is it
这还不…	this is of course…
这有什么不…	what's so (difficult); it's no big deal
只好	have to; forced to; have no other alternative but to
自 (从) …以来	(ever) since…

在…上
on, at

1. 在会上，他说了很多。

   At the meeting, he spoke a lot.

2. 在回家的车上，他想了很多。

   On his way driving home, he thought a lot.

在…下
on (the ground); at

1. 在地下他看见有头发。

   He saw some hair on the ground.

2. 在年下的时候，我们都不上学。

   None of us goes to school at the end of the year.

在…中
in the middle of; in; among; throughout

1. 在家中我是老三。

   I'm the third child in the family.

2. 在一年中这几天很好。

   Of the whole year, these are fine days.

133

一…就
as soon as
1. 我一上车就看见他。
   I saw him as soon as I got on the vehicle.

2. 我一回家就看小说。
   I read novels as soon as I get home.

这不/这不是
Isn't it? / is it?
1. "我的车不见了。""这不？"
   "My car disappeared." "Isn't it here?"

2. "你看见我的小工没有？""这不是？"
   "Did you see my young worker?" "Isn't he here?"

这有什么不…
what's so (difficult); it's no big deal
1. 这有什么不会的，看一下就会了。
   What's so difficult about it. One look and you'll be able to do it.

2. 这有什么不可以说的，大家都知道了。
   Why can't we say it? Anybody knows it.

…就
…all right
1. 你要我说我就说。
   If you want me to say it, I'll say it.

2. 他做就他做吧。
   If he wants to do it, let him do it.

那还用说
needless to say

1. 那还用说，他们以后就和好了。

   Needless to say, they got well together again.

2. 那还用说，他以后就开车去见他了。

   Needless to say, he drove to see him after that.

和…一样
is the same as

1. 中国和你的国家一样。

   China is the same as your country.

2. 我的家人和你的家人一样。

   My family is the same as yours.

以上
above; more than

1. 工人在十六岁以上就可以进工会。

   Workers above 16 years of age can join the union.

2. 三人以上不可以进去。

   More than three people can't enter.

以下
under; less than; fewer than

1. 十个工人以下做不成这事。

   Fewer than ten workers can't accomplish such work.

2. 三小时以下他还不会到这里。

   He wouldn't be able to get here in less than three hours.

以前
before; ...ago; below
1. 四天以前他还在这里。
   He was here four days ago.

2. 工人六十以前都可以做工。
   All of the workers below 60 years of age can work.

以后
after; later
1. 开学以后，大家都来了。
   After the term had begun, we all came back.

2. 回家以后，他就吃起面来。
   After coming home, he ate noodles.

不是…就是…
either...or...
1. 他不是工头就是地主。
   He's either the foreman or the landlord.

2. 你不是老大就是老二。
   You're either the eldest or the second eldest.

就是
right there is
1. 那就是他家老头。
   Right there is the old man in his home.

2. 那就是我的大学。
   Right there is my university.

没有…就没有…
without...there would be no...

1. 没有小学，就没有中学。

   Without primary school, there would be no secondary school.

2. 没有老的，就没有小的。

   Without the old, there would be no young ones.

前十数十量
(past ; last; before; ago) + (number) + (classifier)

1. 前三年我回去过中国。

   I've been to China in these past three years.

2. 上一回我回去过年。

   The last time, I went home for the New Year.

为了…起见
for the sake of; in order to; because of

1. 为了国家和好起见，他只好做下去。

   In order to achieve national harmony, he had to continue his service.

2. 为了一家和好起见，我只得回家。

   For the sake of restoring good relations in the family, I had to go back home.

为了
for, in order to

1. 为了一家大小，我要去做工。

   For the young and old in the family, I had to go and work.

2. 为了见他，我要在这里下车。

   In order to see him, I'm alighting here.

不只…还
not only...but also

1. 我来中国，不只是要开会，还要上学。

   I did not only come to China for the conference, but also to attend school.

2. 我在这里，不只是要看，还要吃。

   I did not only come here to have a look, but to eat as well.

可…的
...able or ...ible/which can be...

1.
可说的	可吃的	可见的
that can be said	edible	visible
可用的	可学的	可要的
usable	that can be learned	that can be wanted/gotten
可想的	可做的	可动的
thinkable	that can be done	movable
可得的	可看的	可进的
obtainable	that can be looked at	that can be entered
可到的		
that can be reached		

worth FV + ing

1. 我家里可吃的很多。

   I have a lot of things worth eating at my home.

2. 我明天可做的事好多好多。

   I have a great deal of work worth doing tomorrow.

从…说起
begin FV + ing from

1. 我们就从"去中国"说起。

   Let's begin (the discussion) from the trip to China.

2. 大家从二十年以前说起。

Everybody began recollecting from twenty years ago.

就是这么来的
this is how it happened/took place/came about

1. "天地会"的会头就是这么来的。

This is how the leader of the Tiandihui* came to be.

2. 我们家的家用就是这么来的。

This is how the family appliances came to be acquired.

从…起
from; since

1. 从一九九四年起，十六以上的工人都可以进工会。

From 1994 onwards, any worker above 16 years of age can join the union.

2. 从小学的时候起，我就看小说。

I've been reading novels since I was in primary school.

从…来
come from

1. 他从家里来。

He came from home.

2. 我从中国来。

I came from China.

只好
have to; forced to

1. 我来看他，可是他不在，我只好走了。

I came to see him. Since he wasn't in, I have no choice but to leave.

*Tiandihui: a secret society formed in early Qing Dynasty.

2. 工地还没开工，我只好过一天来。

Work had not started on the construction site, so I had to come the next day.

自（从）…以来
(ever) since…

1. 自开学以来，他就没来过。

Ever since the beginning of the new term, he hasn't been here.

2. 自从一九九四年以来，他就不在家。

Since 1994, he hasn't been home.

从…去
from...to

1. 从这里去你家只要一小时。

It only takes an hour from here to your home.

2. 从工地开车去你家也是一小时。

It's also an hour's drive from the worksite to your home.

从来没有
has/have never

1. 他从来没有去过中国。

He's never been to China.

2. 他从来没有吃过面。

He's never eaten noodles.

从来不
never

1. 我从来不说人家的不是。

I've never said that anybody is at fault.

2. 他从来不想上学。

He's never wanted to go to school.

…多了
more than; over; much more

1. 他有六十多了。

He's over 60.

2. 这几年他老多了。

He has aged much more over the past few years.

不到
less than; under; not yet

1. 他还不到十六。

He's under 16.

2. 不到十四，不可以进大学。

Anyone under 14 can't enrol for university.

不过
yet; but

1. 他人小，不过心不小。

He's young but very ambitious.

2. 这是他的家，不过他不在里面。

This is his home, but he isn't in.

16. Positive, Negative and Interrogative Sentences

	Positive	Negative	Interrogative
1.	你会。 You can.	我不会。 I can't.	他会不会？ Can he?
2.	你吃。 You eat.	我不吃。 I don't eat.	他吃不吃？ Does he eat?
3.	你说。 You say it.	我不说。 I don't say it.	他说不说？ Does he say it?
4.	你去。 You leave/go.	我不去。 I don't leave/go.	他去不去？ Does he leave/go?
5.	你来。 You come.	我不来。 I don't come.	他来不来？ Does he come?
6.	你走。 You go.	我不走。 I don't go.	他走不走？ Does he go?
7.	你看。 You look.	我不看。 I don't look.	他看不看？ Does he look?
8.	你做。 You do it.	我不做。 I don't do it.	他做不做？ Does he do it?
9.	你用。 You use it.	我不用。 I don't use it.	他用不用？ Does he use it?
10.	你学。 You learn it.	我不学。 I don't learn it.	他学不学？ Does he learn it?
11.	你想。 You think.	我不想。 I don't think.	他想不想？ Does he think?
12.	你是。 You are	我不是。 I'm not.	他是不是？ Is he?
13.	你要。 You want it.	我不要。 I don't want it.	他要不要？ Doe he want it?
14.	你动。 You move.	我不动。 I don't move.	他动不动？ Does he move?

15.	你打。	我不打。	他打不打？
	You hit it.	I don't hit it.	Does he hit it?
16.	你好。	我不好。	他好不好？
	You're all right.	I'm not all right.	Is he all right?
17.	你在。	我不在。	他在不在？
	You're in.	I'm not in.	Is he in?
18.	你成。	我不成。	他成不成？
	You can do it.	I can't do it.	Can he do it?
19.	你对。	我不对。	他对不对？
	You're right.	I'm not right.	Is he right?
20.	你出。	我不出。	他出不出？
	You exit.	I don't exit.	Does he exit?
21.	你进。	我不进。	他进不进？
	You enter.	I don't enter.	Does he enter?
22.	你有。	我没有。	他有没有？
	You have it.	I don't have it.	Does he have it?
23.	你行。	我不行。	他行不行？
	You can do it.	I can't do it.	Can he do it?
24.	你老。	我不老。	他老不老？
	You're old.	I'm not old.	Is he old?
25.	你回。	我不回。	他回不回？
	You go back.	I don't go back.	Does he go back?
26.	你知。	我不知。	他知不知？
	You know it.	I don't know it.	Does he know it?

17. "你 (You)，我(I)，他 (He)，我们 (We)" and "也 (Too)，都 (All)" Sentences

1. 你有家。   You have a home.
    我有家。   I have a home.
    他也有家。   He too has a home.
    我们都有家。   We all have a home.

2. 你有车。   You have a car.
    我有车。   I have a car.
    他也有车。   He too has a cars.
    我们都有车。   We all have a car.

3. 你有事。   You have something on.
    我有事。   I have something on.
    他也有事。   He too has something on.
    我们都有事。   We all have something on.

4. 你去做工。   You go to work.
    我去做工。   I go to work.
    他也去做工。   He too goes to work.
    我们都去做工。   We all go to work.

5. 你要开会。   You have a meeting.
    我要开会。   I have a meeting.
    他也要开会。   He too has a meeting.
    我们都要开会。   We all have a meeting.

6. 你要上车。   You're to get into the car.
    我要上车。   I'm going to get into the car.

他也要上车。 He too wants to get into the car.
我们都要上车。 We all want to get into the car.

7. 你要进去。 You're going in.
   我要进去。 I'm going in.
   他也要进去。 He too is going in.
   我们都要进去。 We're all going in.

8. 你要过来。 You're coming over.
   我要过来。 I'm coming over.
   他也要过来。 He too is coming over.
   我们都要过来。 We're all coming over.

9. 你要看。 You want to see it.
   我要看。 I want to see it.
   他也要看。 He too wants to see it.
   我们都要看。 We all want to see it.

10. 你要学。 You want to learn.
    我要学。 I want to learn.
    他也要学。 He too wants to learn.
    我们都要学。 We all want to learn.

11. 你要走。 You want to go.
    我要走。 I want to go.
    他也要走。 He too wants to go.
    我们都要走。 We all want to go.

12. 你要吃。 You want to eat.
    我要吃。 I want to eat.
    他也要吃。 He too wants to eat.
    我们都要吃。 We all want to eat.

13. 你要说。 You want to talk.
    我要说。 I want to talk.

他也要说。	He too wants to talk.
我们都要说。	We all want to talk.

14.
你要做工。	You want to work.
我要做工。	I want to work.
他也要做工。	He too wants to work.
我们都要做工。	We all want to work.

15.
你要回家。	You want to go home.
我要回家。	I want to go home.
他也要回家。	He too wants to go home.
我们都要回家。	We all want to go home.

16.
你要开工。	You want to start working.
我要开工。	I want to start working.
他也要开工。	He too wants to start working.
我们都要开工。	We all want to start working.

17.
你要动工。	You want to commence the job.
我要动工。	I want to commence the job.
他也要动工。	He too wants to commence the job.
我们都要动工。	We all want to commence the job.

18.
你要上进。	You want to improve yourself.
我要上进。	I want to improve myself.
他也要上进。	He too wants to improve himself.
我们都要上进。	We all want to improve ourselves.

19.
你要上学。	You want to go to school.
我要上学。	I want to go to school.
他也要上学。	He too wants to go to school.
我们都要上学。	We all want to go to school.

20.
你要做事。	You want to do something.
我要做事。	I want to do something.
他也要做事。	He too wants to do something.
我们都要做事。	We all want to do something.

18. Sentence Pyramids

好
很好
做得很好
你做得很好
这事你做得很好
这事你们做得很好
这事你们大家都做得很好
Good.
Very good.
Very well done.
You did it very well.
You have done this very well.
You have done this very well.
Everyone of you have done it very well.

来
来回
来来回回
车子来来回回
很多车子来来回回
很多车子来来回回地走
很多大车和小车来来回回地走
Come.
Come and go.
Coming and going.
Cars are coming and going.
Many cars are coming and going.
Many cars are coming and going about.
Many big and small cars are coming and going about.

不
不要
不要吃
不要吃面
我不要吃面
我不要吃这么多面
我不要吃这么多的面
No.
Don't want to.
Don't want to eat.
Don't want to eat noodles.
I don't want to eat noodles.
I don't want to eat so much noodles.
I don't want to eat such a lot of noodles.

做
做事
做好事
那个人做好事
那个人做了好事
那个人做了很多好事
那个人做了很多很好的事
Do.
Do things.
Do good things.
That person does good deeds.
That person has done good deeds.
That person has done many good deeds.
That person has done a lot of good deeds.

学
自己学
自己要学
自己要用心学
自己要用心地学
我们自己要用心地学
我们自己要很用心地学

Learn.

Learn yourself.

Want to learn yourself.

One must learn attentively.

One must be attentive to learn.

All of us have to learn attentively.

All of us have to learn very attentively.

老
老人
老人家
他老人家
他老人家是个好人
他老人家是个做很多好事的人
他老人家是个做很多好事的大好人

Old.

Old man.

Old folks.

He's an old man.

He's a good old man.

He's a good old man who does many good deeds.

He's a very good old man who does a lot of good deeds.

走
我走
我和他走
我和他一起走
我和他一起走回家
我和他一起走回老家
我和他一起走回我们的老家
Go.
I'll go.
He and I'll go.
I'll go with him.
He and I go home together.
He and I visit our hometown together.
He and I go back to our hometown together.

我
我的
我的事
我的事情
这是我的事情
这是我主要的事情
这是我主要要做的事情
I.
Mine.
My business.
My business.
This is my business.
This is my main business.
This is the main business I want to do.

看
看来
看起来
看起来很可口
看起来还很可口
这看起来是很可口的
看起来这是很可口的面

Look.

Looks like.

Looks as if.

Looks as if it were tasty.

Looks as if it could be tasty.

This looks as if it were very tasty.

It looks as if they were very tasty noodles.

要
要不要？
要不要上学？
明天要不要上学？
明天要不要和我一起上学？
明天要不要和我们一起上学？
明天你要不要和我们一起开车去上学？

Want.

Do you want to?

Do you want to go to school?

Do you want to go to school tomorrow?

Do you want to go to school with me tomorrow?

Do you want to go to school with us tomorrow?

Do you want to go to school with us by car tomorrow?

他
他好学
他很好学
他多么好学
他是个多么好学的人
他自小就是个好学的人
他自小就是一个好学的人

He.

He's studious.

He's very studious.

How studious he is!

What a studious person he is.

He has been studious since childhood.

He is a person who has been studious since childhood.

下
下车
我要下车
我要下车了
我要下车去了
我要在这里下车了
我就要在这里下车了

Down.

Alight.

I'm getting out of the car.

I'm getting out of the car.

I'm going to get out of the car.

I'm going to get out of the car here.

I'm going to get out of the car just here.

说
说得多
你说得很多
你说来说去说得很多
你说来说去还是说得不对
你说来说去说了那么多还是不对
你一五一十地说来说去说了那么多还是不对

Say.
Say a lot.
You've said a lot.
You've rambled on and on and said a lot.
You've said a lot but you've still not said it right.
You've said so much but you've still not said it right.
You've said it in full detail but you've still not said it right.

开
开心
我很开心
我现在很开心
我现在多么开心
我现在是多么的开心
我现在的心情是多么的开心

Open.
Feel happy.
I'm very happy.
I'm very happy now.
How happy I'm now.
Right now I'm feeling very happy.
What a happy mood I'm in now.

心
心地
心地好
他的人心地好
他为人心地很好
他的为人就是心地好
他到头来还是一个心地很好的人
Heart.

Moral nature.

Kind-hearted.

He is kind-hearted.

He is such a kind-hearted person.

He is just such a kind-hearted person.

He is a kind-hearted person in every way.

发明
发明家
他是一个发明家
他是一个中国的发明家
他是一个来自中国的发明家
他是个发明家，也是个小说家
他是个来自中国的发明家，又是个小说家
Invent.

Inventor.

He is an inventor.

He is a Chinese inventor.

He is an inventor from China.

He is both an inventor and a novelist.

He is both an inventor and a novelist from China.

老

老头

老头子

老头子上车

老头子自己上车

老头子自己一个人上车

老头子自己一个人上去车里面

Old.

Old man.

Old man/old chap.

The old man gets in a car.

The old man gets in a car by himself.

The old man gets in a car all by himself.

The old man gets inside the car all by himself.

动

动心

他动心了

他看见就动心了

他一看见你就动心了

他一看见你就那么动心

为什么他一看见你就那么动心？

Move.

Moved emotionally.

He is moved emotionally.

He is moved at the sight of it.

He is moved at the sight of you.

He is so moved at the sight of you.

Why is he so moved at the sight of you?

出

出国

出国去

我要出国去

我要出国去看看

我要出国到中国去看看

我明年要出国到中国去看看

Go out.

Go abroad.

Go abroad.

I want to go abroad.

I want to go abroad to see what it's like.

I want to go to China to see what it's like.

I want to go to China next year to see what it's like.

用

用一用

想用一用

想用一用车

他想用一用车去上工

他明天想用一用车去上工

他明天想用一用车到工地去上工

Use.

Use for a while.

Consider using for a while.

Consider using a car for a while.

He's considering using the car to go to work.

He's considering taking the car to work tomorrow.

He's considering taking the car to the worksite for work tomorrow.

事
心事
心里的事
他心里有事
他有很多心事
他有很不开心的事
他天天都有很多不开心的事

Thing.

Something on one's mind.

Something weighing on one's mind.

He has something weighing on his mind.

He has a lot of things weighing on his mind.

He has something very unpleasant weighing on his mind.

He has a lot of unpleasant things weighing on his mind every day.

主
自主
自主国
自主的国家
自己做主的国家
自己可以做主的国家
自己可以做自己主人的国家

Self.

Own decision

Independent country.

Independent country.

A nation which acts on its own.

A nation which can decide for itself.

A nation whose people can be their own masters.

想
想家
我想家
我很想家
我很想我的家
我很想我的老家
我很想我老家的人

Miss.

Miss home.

I miss home.

I miss home very much.

I miss my home very much.

I miss my hometown very much.

I miss the people in my hometown very much.

说
说一说
想说一说
他想说一说
他想说一说工地的事
他想说一说工地上的事情
他想说一说工地上明天要做的事情

Speak.

Mention.

Want to say something.

He wants to say something.

He wants to talk about things of the worksite.

He wants to talk about things on the worksite.

He wants to talk about things to be done tomorrow on the worksite.

回
回家
我回家
我要回家
明年我要回家
明年我要回家去
明年我就要回家去了

Return.

Return home.

I return home.

I want to return home.

I want to return home next year.

I want to go back home next year.

I'm going to return home next year.

看
看一看
想看一看
想看一看我的家
想看一看我在那里的家
想看一看我在那里的家人
我想看一看我在那里的家人

Look/see.

Have a look.

Want to have a look.

Want to have a look at my home.

Want to have a look at my home there.

Want to have a look at my family there.

I want to have a look at my family there.

19. Alternatives of "He is a good man"

1. 他很好。
   He's good.

2. 他是好人。
   He's a good man.

3. 他是个好人。
   He's a good man.

4. 他是很好的人。
   He's a very good man.

5. 他人好的很。
   As a person he's very good.

6. 他人很好的。
   As a person he's very good.

7. 他是一个很好的人。
   He's a very good man.

8. 他心好。
   He's a kind-hearted man.

9. 他心地好。
   He's a kind-hearted man.

10. 他的心很好。
    He has a kind heart.

11. 他是个心地很好的人。
    He's a kind-hearted person.

12. 他是个好心人。
    He's a kind person.

13. 他为人很好。
    As a person he's very good.

14. 他为人好得很。
    As a person he's very good.

15. 他是那么好的一个人。
    He's that kind person.

16. 他是这样好的一个人。
    He's such a nice person.

17. 他是个这样好的人。
    He's a such nice person.

18. 他是个少见的好人。
    He's such a rare and nice person.

19. 他是个不可多得的好人。
    There's seldom such a nice person as him.

20. 他的人好是很好，不过…
    As a person, he's very kind, but…

20. Descriptions of a Man

1. 他是个成年人。
    He's an adult.

2. 他是个中年人。
    He's a middle-aged man.

3. 他是个老年人。
    He's an old-aged man.

4. 他是个老人。
    He's an old man.

5. 他是个老头。
    He's an old chap.

6. 他是个老头子。
    He's an old chap

7. 他是个回回。
    He's a muslim.

8. 他是个出家人。
    He's a monk.

9. 他是个多情的人。
    He's an emotional person.

10. 他是个好看的人。
    He's a good-looking man.

11. 他是个口吃的人。
    He stutters.

12. 他是个会开车的人。
   He's a person who can drive.

13. 他是个要面子的人。
   He's a person to whom face is important.

14. 他是个工人。
   He's a worker.

15. 他是个打工的人。
   He's a labourer.

16. 他是个地主。
   He's a landlord.

17. 他是个工头。
   He's a foreman.

18. 他是过来人。
   He's a man who has experience in this respect.

19. 他是个小心的人。
   He's a cautious person.

20. 他是个没家小的人。
   He's a man without a family.

21. 他是那个人的心上人。
   He's a sweetheart of that person.

22. 他是那个人的情人。
   He's a lover of that person.

23. 他是个大吃的人。
   He's a man who eats a lot.

24. 他是个大个子。
    He's a man of great built.

25. 他是个小个子。
    He's a man of small built.

26. 他是个好动的人。
    He's an active person.

27. 他是自己人。
    He's one of us.

28. 他是中人。
    He's a middle man.

29. 他老是和人不对头。
    He always goes against other people's opinions.

30. 他老是和人过不去。
    He can never get along with others well.

31. 他是个对不起人的人。
    He's someone who always exploits others.

32. 他是个自以为是的人。
    He thinks highly of himself.

33. 他是个不三不四的人。
    He's a shady character.

34. 他是个老三老四的人。
    He's a child who likes to imitate adults.

35. 他是个没大没小的人。
    He's a person who has no respect for elders.

164

36. 他是个自我中心的人。
    He's a self-centered person.

37. 他是个看上不看下的人。
    He's snobbish.

38. 他是个看前不看后的人。
    He's a person who cares the front but not the back.

39. 他是个只说不做的人。
    He's a man of words, not a man of action.

40. 他是个只吃不做的人。
    He's a lazy man.

41. 他是个会说不会做的人。
    He's a man who can only talk but not act.

42. 他是个中看不中用的人。
    He's only good to look at but not of much use.

43. 他是个一去不回头的人。
    He's a man who never looks back.

44. 他是个动不动就打人的人。
    He's a man who resorts to violence.

45. 他是个不中用的人。
    He's a man of little value.

46. 他是个没用的人。
    He's a useless man.

47. 他是个不用心的人。
    He's a careless man.

48. 他是个人在心不在的人。
   He's a man who is present physically but not in attention.

49. 他是个成天有心事的人。
   He's a man who is obsessed with his problems.

50. 他是个很有成见的人。
   He's a very opinionated man.

51. 他是个自大的人。
   He's an arrogant person.

52. 他是个好吃的人。
   He's a greedy person.

53. 他是个好事的人。
   He's a busybody.

54. 他是个不会开口的人。
   He's a man who rarely opens his mouth.

55. 他是个想不开的人。
   He's a man who takes things too seriously.

56. 他是个不会动心的人。
   He's a man who is hardly touched/moved.

57. 他是个多心的人。
   He's over-sensitive.

58. 他是个了不得的人。
   He's a remarkable person.

59. 他是个不得了的人。
   He's an extraordinary person.

60. 他是个出人头地的人。
He stands out among his peers.

61. 他是个不可多得的人。
He's a person hard to come by.

62. 他是个有成就的人。
He's an accomplished man.

63. 他是个经得起大事的人。
He's a person who can handle heavy responsibilities.

64. 他是个为国家做大事的人。
He's a man who does important things for the country.

65. 他是个为国为家的人。
He's a man for both the nation and the people.

66. 他是个主要的人。
He's an important person.

67. 他是个主动的人。
He's an active person.

68. 他是个自动的人。
He's a man with initiative.

69. 他是个自动自发的人。
He's a man with initiative and spontaneity.

70. 他是个有头有面的人。
He's a reputable person.

71. 他是个明了事情的人。
He's an understanding person.

72. 他是个很有心地的人。
He's a man with morality and ethics.

73. 他是个开明的人。
He's an open-minded person.

74. 他是个开心的人。
He's a light-hearted person.

75. 他是个有心的人。
He's a very attentive man.

76. 他是个要上进的人。
He wants to improve himself all the time.

77. 他是个好学的人。
He's keen on learning.

78. 他是个有用的人。
He's a useful person.

79. 他是个大面子的人。
He's a man who is important and influencial.

80. 他是个大有可为的人。
He's a person who has bright prospects.

81. 他是个大得人心的人。
He's a very popular person.

82. 他是个老成的人。
He's very mature.

83. 他是个老好人。
He's an honest man not likely to harm others.

168

84. 他是个样样都会的人。
    He's a very versatile person.

85. 他是个前进的人。
    He's a forward-looking man.

86. 他是个要人。
    He's an VIP.

87. 他是个国家的要人。
    He's the State's VIP.

88. 他是个想什么就说什么的人。
    He's a man who says what he means.

89. 他是个说得到做得到的人。
    He's a man who does what he preaches.

90. 他是个和事老。
    He's a peace-maker.

91. 他是个见不得人的人。
    He's a shameful person.

92. 他是我的知心人。
    He's my bosom friend.

93. 他是我的意中人。
    He's my lover.

94. 他是个少年人。
    He's a teenager.

95. 他是个 (gè) 中 (zhōng) 人。
    He's in the know.

21. 100 Idioms

1. 一是一，二是二
   One is one, and two is two – call a spade a spade; honest.

2. 一五一十
   In full detail.

3. 一家大小
   The whole family including old and young.

4. 一家和好
   A cordial and harmonious family.

5. 一来二去
   In the course of contacts.

6. 一前一后
   Arranged one in the front, the other at the back.

7. 一年到头
   Throughout the year.

8. 一分为二
   One divided into two.

9. 七七八八
   Almost completed.

10. 七上八下
    Be agitated; be perturbed; at sixes and sevens.

11. 七老八十
The age of 70–80.

12. 七十二行
All kinds of trades, occupations and businesses.

13. 十不得一
Out of ten cases, not even one success.

14. 十之八九
Eight or nine cases (out of ten); very likely to succeed; 80 to 90 per cent chance of success.

15. 十有八九
(same as above).

16. 人老心不老
Old in age but still young at heart.

17. 人小心不小
Young in age but ambitious at heart.

18. 人到中年
A person reaching middle age.

19. 人前人后
A person who knows how to behave towards others always.

20. 人在人情在
Sentiment exists as long as we are alive.

21. 人人为我，我为人人
All for one and one for all.

22. 上上下下
   The separation of high and low, young and old, up and down.

23. 上下一心
   From top to bottom, young and old, everyone with the same goal.

24. 三三五五
   Groups of three or five.

25. 了不可见
   Cannot see clearly.

26. 了了可见
   To see every detail clearly.

27. 小中见大
   To see the major from the minor, the important from trivial.

28. 小心从事
   To be careful and cautious in doing things.

29. 小小天地
   A small world of one's own.

30. 小时了了
   A child being clever beyond his age.

31. 大得人心
   To win people's hearts; to be very popular.

32. 大有人在
   There are plenty of such people; such people are by no means rare.

33. 大有可为

To be well worth doing; to have bright prospects.

34. 大有见地

To have valuable opinions or views.

35. 口到心到

To learn meaning of a word through pronunciation and speech.

36. 不三不四

Dubious; neither one nor the other.

37. 不上不下

Neither up nor down.

38. 不大不小

Neither big nor small; just nice.

39. 不了了之

To shelve the matter; dealing with a problem without end.

40. 不得人心

To be unpopular with people; fail to gain people's favour.

41. 不得不说

To have no other alternative but to say it out.

42. 不可多得

Hard to come by; rare.

43. 不得已为之

To have no alternative but to do it.

44. 从小到大
    From young to old; small to big.

45. 从上到下
    From up to down; from head to toe; from top to bottom.

46. 从头做起
    To do something from the very beginning.

47. 心口不一
    Not doing what one preaches; not saying what one thinks.

48. 心想事成
    Accomplish what one wishes; set one's mind on something.

49. 心不二用
    One mind can't concentrate on two things.

50. 为之心动
    Motivated to act.

51. 天下大事
    Important world affairs.

52. 见不得人
    Something shameful; too ashamed to face other people.

53. 少年老成
    Young but looks mature.

54. 中看不中用
    Good to look at but not useful.

55. 可大可小
    Adjustable; can be either big or small.

174

56. 出人头地
   To stand out among one's fellows.

57. 只事一主
   To be loyal only to one's master.

58. 头头是道
   Clear and logical.

59. 对人对事
   To deal with people and matters simultaneously; to be subjective.

60. 对事不对人
   To deal with matters only and not the person; to be objective.

61. 自动自发
   Voluntarily; spontaneously.

62. 自成一家
   In Art, to have a style of one's own; to be unique in one's style.

63. 自以为是
   To regard oneself as infallible; to be opinionated.

64. 自知之明
   Self-knowledge; self-awareness.

65. 自我中心
   Self-centred.

66. 自在自得
   Self-complacent; self-satisfied.

67. 自在人心
Known to everybody; self-evident.

68. 有样学样
To follow or imitate someone else.

69. 有一得一
To take whatever is available.

70. 有头有面
Reputable; recognized.

71. 有什么，说什么
To be frank; straightforward.

72. 成事在天
Success depends on chance or fate.

73. 成为知己
To become bosom friends.

74. 好自为之
To watch one's own behaviour.

75. 好人好事
Good persons and deeds.

76. 来来回回
Comings and goings.

77. 来来去去
Comings and goings.

78. 来回来去
To come and go; back and forth.

79. 来头不小

A respectable or powerful person or family.

80. 老大不小

Old enough to know or do.

81. 老老少少

The young and old; everybody.

82. 老来得子

One who fathers a son in old age.

83. 老三老四

A child who imitates a grown-up's behaviour.

84. 没大没小

To be impolite to an elder (there should be ranking according to the Chinese custom).

85. 知人之明

Able to appreciate a person's character and capability.

86. 知人知面不知心

Knowing a person's face does not mean knowing his heart; never judge by appearance.

87. 知之为知之，不知为不知，是知也

If you know, you know that you know; but if you do not know, you must admit that you do not.

88. 事在人为

All things depend on human effort.

89. 事不得已

One has no alternative.

90. 看前看后
Look both ahead and behind.

91. 国家大事
The State's affairs.

92. 国之大老
An aged person who has made great contributions to the country.

93. 学到老学不了
One never stops learning; there is much to learn.

94. 说到做到
To do what one has said; to keep one's promise.

95. 说三道四
Gossip; shop talk.

96. 说一不二
To mean what one says; stand by one's word.

97. 前前后后
From beginning to end; the front and the back.

98. 家有一老
It's a pleasure to have an elder in the family.

99. 想前想后
To think of consequences; think twice.

100. 要什么，有什么
To have whatever one wants; to be lucky.

22. **300 Short Sentences**

A. Time

1. 几点了？你知道现在几点了？我想我得回家
    了。
    What's the time? Do you know the time? I think I'd better be
    going home.

2. 什么时候了？我要走了，你还有什么事没有？
    What's the time? I've to go. Is there anything else?

3. 五点四十分了，他已经走了吧？
    It's already 5.40 p.m. Has he gone yet?

4. 那还用说？三点二十分开会，大家都得到，一
    个人也不可以少！
    Need it be said? The meeting is at 3.20 p.m. and all must be
    present. No one is to be absent.

5. 还有二十分就到十二点了，怎么他还没有回
    家？你知道他会去我们工头那里不？
    Another twenty minutes and it'll be twelve o'clock. Why is
    he not back yet? Has he gone to see our foreman?

6. 对不起，我来得不是时候。
    I'm sorry. I've come at the wrong time.

7. 好吧，我看就这样做吧。那么点事，一天就做
    好了，要不了三天。
    All right, I think we'll do it this way. It's only a small job and
    it can be finished in a day. There is no need for three days.

8. 三个人做五天和五个人做三天，还不都是一样？

Three men do a job in five days, and five men do it in three days. Aren't they the same thing?

9. 要是你打从这里过去，不出三天就可以到。

If you go by this way, you'll get there within three days.

10. 这已经是三天以前的事了，你不会不知道吧？

This happened three days ago. Surely you must know about it!

11. 天还没明，可是出工的时候到了，大家都出发去上工。

Morning hasn't arrived but it's time for work. Everyone is leaving for work.

12. 从我国到中国，只要八小时就可以打个来回。

It takes only eight hours to make a return trip from here to China.

13. 他这时候还不来，我看他十之八九是来不了了！

He still hasn't come by now. I don't think he'll make it.

14. 这几天，有时天好，有时天不好。

During these few days, the weather has been fluctuating between good and bad.

15. 他说他要明天去，不，后天去。

He said he would go tomorrow, no, sorry, the day after tomorrow.

16. 他三天来一回，你一天来三回。
He comes every three days, whereas you come three times a day.

17. 都到这时候了，我想我不得不说了。
I don't think I should remain silent any longer at this point.

18. 他小的时候从中国来，到现在也过了二十多年，还没有回去过。
He came from China when he was a child. He has been here for over twenty years already but he hasn't gone back to China at all.

19. 我家的老大明年十九了，老二也要进中学了，还有个老三，还在上小学。
My oldest child will be nineteen years old next year. The second will be going to secondary school, and the third is still in primary school.

20. 说他小也不小，大也不大，去年过了十七，这回有十八九了，还没有上大学！
He can't be considered young, but neither can he be considered old. He was seventeen years old last year. He's close to nineteen years old now but he has still not entered university.

21. 都十七八九成年人了，还老是做不三不四的事情，不成个样子！
He's almost twenty years old but he's still doing silly things. He's definitely not a model young man.

22. 他看起来多么好看，不见得是个六十出头的人吧？
He looks really good. It's unbelievable that he's over sixty years old.

23. 他看不出有四十了，我还以为他只有三十！
He doesn't look like he's forty. I thought he was only thirty years old!

24. 这几年他看上去老多了，事情不好做，他心上的事都做不成。人是个老好人，五十看来有六十的。
He has aged during these few years. Things have not gone well with him. Whatever he did didn't turn out successful. He's a nice man. Although he's fifty years old, he looks sixty.

25. 你说他有五十大几。不会，不会，看来只不过四十多。
Did you say he's in his late fifties? It can't be. He looks like he's only in his forties.

26. 这人看上去有三十出头，可是还没成家。
He looks like he's over thirty, but he's still not married.

27. 这是个四十上下的中年人，我上上下下地看过了他。我说："就这样好了，你回去想想，我也回去想想，想过以后，我们明天可以见个面，你说好不好？"
He's in his forties. I looked him from head to toe and said, "We'll leave the matter as this. You go home and think it over. I'll do the same. Then we'll meet tomorrow. What do you say?"

28. 他老人家七十出头了，开车一样看得见，一样开得那么好。
That old man is over seventy but he can still drive very well. He can see well too.

182

29. 人老了，不中用了，这样小的事也做不成。
When we get old we become useless. We can't even do a small thing.

30. 这事你可不要说出去，人家老人知道了，会不开心的。
You mustn't tell anyone about this. If his father gets to know about it, he won't be happy.

B.　Daily Living

1. 都三点了，你还没吃吧？要不要吃点点心？
It's already three o'clock and you still haven't eaten. Do you want some snacks?

2. 这里什么都有：吃的、用的、看的什么的，你要怎么样都可以。
Everything that you want is available here: food, tools, ornaments etc. You can do whatever pleases you.

3. 你在这里，吃的、用的都是现成的，自己人，不用想那么多。
You're here among friends. Please help yourself to the food and anything that you want. Don't stand on ceremony.

4. 吃吧，又吃不下；不吃吧，主人会不开心。
The food is unpalatable, yet I might offend the host, if I don't eat it.

5. 他吃了面就走了，也不回头看看他老人家。
After eating the noodles, he left. He didn't even look back at his father.

6. "你吃好了没有？吃好就要上学了。"
   "我吃好了，现在到你吃了。"
   "Have you finished eating? You should be leaving for school now."
   "I've finished. It's now your turn to eat."

7. 我吃不了很多，要是前面有小吃也成。
   I don't want to eat too much. Some snacks will do.

8. "家里有什么吃的没有？有什么好吃的？我还没吃过！"
   "Is there anything good to eat in the house? I've not eaten yet."

9. 你是什么时候发的面？三个小时以前吧。
   When did you leaven the bread? Was it three hours ago?

10. 他心里有事不要说，成天不吃不做的，看样子就要不中用了。
    He keeps all his problems to himself. He hasn't been eating and doing anything. He looks as if he's wasting away.

11. 你还没有吃过可可，要不要吃吃看？很好吃的。
    You haven't tasted cocoa before. Would you like to try some? It's delicious.

12. 你看，面发起来了，你想吃什么就说吧，要不要现在就做？
    Look, the dough has risen. Tell me what you'd like to eat. Do you want to eat now?

184

13. 这年头好人好事多起来了，前天我还看见有人
    为一个出家人做面吃。
    This year has seen many volunteer workers. The day before
    yesterday I saw a volunteer cooking noodles for a monk.

14. 走，去看看那里有什么好吃的。
    Come, let's go and see what good things there are to eat.

15. 我们都吃过了，你自己吃好了。
    All of us have eaten. You'll have to eat by yourself.

16. 他这个人，对我来说，是可有可无的。也就是
    说，没有他，我也可以过得一样好。
    To me, he's of no importance, that's I can live as well
    without him.

17. 他不是已经说过"对不起"了？说过就行了，
    小事情，过去就没事了。
    Hasn't he apologised already? It's only a small matter, let it
    rest.

18. 这几天我要做的人情多得很，这里要人情，那
    里要人情，在在都要用到大头*。这下子我可
    过不去了。
    These few days I've received many invitations. The gifts for
    all these occasions are costing me a lot of money.

19. "你面子大，你老人家为我说说情去。"
    "You're an influential person. Please put in a good word for
    me."

* 大头 : silver coin

20. 这事得他出面才行，一来他面子大，二来他是个过来人。

He has to deal with it. For one thing, he's an influential person. He also has the experience.

21. 他来得了，来不了，我说不上。

I can't confirm whether he's able to come or not.

22. 他说他的，我做我的。

He says what he wants and I just carry on with what I want to do.

23. 他不是不要说，是说不得，有的事可以说，有的事不可以说，他想前想后，以为还是不说的好。

It is not that he doesn't want to say it. He can't say it. Some things can be said while others can't. He has thought it over and has decided not to say it.

24. 只要大家过得好，天国就在这里。

Paradise is leading a happy life.

25. 你说中了，你说"他这个人自大得不得了，有一天他会过不去的"，你看他现在可不是上又上不得，下又下不来！

You said that his arrogance would land him in trouble one day. Well, it has come true. He's in trouble now.

26. 在车上的十七八个人，说的说，看的看，大家都那么开心。

There were seventeen or eighteen people on the bus. Some were talking while others were looking at the scenery. Everyone was having a good time.

27. 他回过头来，对后面的下人说："我没事了，现在好好的，回过来了，你们可以走了。"

He turned around and said to his servant, "I'm all right now. I've recovered. You may go now."

28. 只要大家和好，什么事都做得成。

As long as the whole family live harmoniously, anything can be accomplished.

29. 为什么？为什么见不得人？你又不是没头没面的人？

Why? Why are you ashamed of yourself? You're a person of integrity, aren't you?

30. "他想吃我？没那么好的事！我要他好看，看他吃不吃得过去！"

He wants to bully me. No way. I'll show him. Let's see if he can bully me then.

31. "家里有没有人？""有没有人在家？"他这样说了好几回，我这时说又不是，不说又不是,我可不要他发现我一个人在人家家里。

"Is anybody home?" He called out repeatedly. I kept quiet all the time because I didn't want him to know that I was alone in the house.

32. 我从车子上头看下来的时候，看见有个工头一面开车，一面在打他的小工，我说："你为什么打人？不可以打人！"可是他想也不想，还是一下又一下地打。

I looked down from my vehicle and saw a foreman beating his worker whilst driving. I called out to the foreman, "Why are you hitting the man? You can't just beat people up." However, he ignored me and continued beating the man.

33. 我打发一个人去看他，可是没有看见他，家里、地里都看不见。

I sent someone to look for him, but he was nowhere to be found. He was neither at home nor in the fields.

34. 想说就说，想做就做，做人这样多好！

If we could say what we thought and do what we liked, how wonderful it would be!

35. 好在这里都是自己人，大家想说什么就说什么好了。

We're all friends so let's speak our mind.

36. 人家都没有说你是个小人，你又为什么要多心？

Nobody has said that you are mean. Don't be so suspicious.

37. 你去我也去，你不去我也不去。我就是要有样学样，学你一个样。

If you go, I'll go; if you don't, I won't either. I just want to follow whatever you do.

38. 这事就是你不说，我也明了。

Even without you saying it, I understand already.

39. 多年没见他了，他还是和从前一个样。

I haven't seen him for a couple of years; he still looks the same.

40. 他是打了你一下，不过他不是有心的。

I know he hit you, but it wasn't intentional.

41. 他这个人，要么不说，一说就说个没了。

He's like this. He either remains silent or talks ceaselessly.

42. 他四下里看了一看，什么人也没看见。
He looked around and saw nobody.

43. 心里想的都不一样，我和他说不到一起，说不来。
We have a totally different perspective towards life. There isn't much we can talk about.

44. 你们走了之后，他就来了，没见到你。
He arrived soon after you all left; of course he didn't see you.

45. 他明里说好，心里想的，不是那么回事。
What he said isn't what he thinks.

46. 以前他老是以自己为中心，"自我中心"得很，不过，现在好多了。
He was a very self-centred person, but this is no more the case.

47. 他又想去又想不去，后来还是没有去。
He was undecided about going. Finally he decided not to go.

48. 他们二人不和，就是打从那时候起的。
Ever since that time, they became enemies.

49. 我的事多，年来和他只见过一、二回面。
I've been very busy. I've only met up with him once or twice this year.

50. 看样子，八成他是不会来的了。
It looks like he won't be coming.

51. 他出国都有十年了，到现在还没见他回来。
He has been abroad for more than ten years. Until now he hasn't returned.

52. 那天我有点事要和你说，这回见到你，又想不起了。
That day I wanted to talk to you about something. But I just can't recall what it is now.

53. 你又不是七老八十的，为什么想不起？
Why can't you recall what it is? You aren't that old!

54. 经你这么一说，我又想起来了。
I suddenly remember what it is while you were speaking.

55. 这一天，家里只有我一个人，大家都出去了。
Today I'm the only one at home. Everyone has gone out.

56. 我回来三天了，去看过你几回，你都不在，这回可见到你了。
I've been back for three days already. I went to your house a couple of times but you weren't in each time. I'm glad we can finally meet up now.

57. 你去为他们说和说和，做个和事老，要不，做个中人也好。
Be a peace-maker and bring them together. Otherwise, act as their mediator.

58. 你几时回来？老人家想你想得很。
When are you coming home? The old man misses you very much.

59. 是的，我们见过一面。不过，那天大家只是
点了点头，没说什么。

Yes, we've met. But that day we just greeted each other causally.

60. 那样好看的头发，为什么只一下子就走了
样？

It was such a beautiful hairdo. What happened to it?

61. 你会自己做头发吧！你这头发是不是自己做
的？可好看了。

You really know how to wear your hair. Did you style your hair yourself? It looks really good.

62. 你看他头发的样子多好，就这么几下子，打
点打点就很好看了。

Look, he's got a really good cut. He doesn't need to do much to make it look good.

63. 他的车是自动的，他可以一面开车，一面和
我说三道四地说个没了。

He has an automatic car which allows him to both drive and chat ceaselessly with me.

64. 这样经用的车子，我还没见过。

I've never come across such a dependable car.

65. 车子一会就开过来了，我们还是一起走，好
不好？

The car will be arriving soon. Let's go together.

66. 那三个人你看我，我看你，什么都没说。

Those three men are just looking at one another. They haven't said a word.

67. 他对我说"回头见"，一下子就不见了。
He said, "See you later" and disappeared.

68. 可好，我要看他，他就来了。
Just when I wanted to see him, he appeared.

69. 他还不来，我只好一个人去了。
He's still not here. I think I'd better go by myself.

70. 他自小说一是一，说二是二，大了，可了不起。
He's always meant what he says since he was young. It's remarkable that he's kept to it in his adulthood.

71. 他从小到大都自以为很了不起，说得多，做得少，是个自大的人。
Since he was a child, he's had a superiority complex. He talks a lot but does very little. He's an arrogant man.

72. 有一天，我走在人行道上，他从后面小心地开车过来，对我说："怎么好几天没见到你了？"
One day as I was walking along the pavement, he pulled up in his car and said, "I haven't seen you for quite some time now."

73. 那天我经过过道时见到他，是不是那个大个子？
I thought I saw him that day as I was passing through the corridor. Isn't he a large person?

74. 他的出发点是好的，只是说得过头了一点，你说是不是？
He started off well, but went overboard later on. Don't you think so?

75. 这回我就做下去，到头看会不会成。
   I'll work on to see if it'll succeed this time.

76. 得了，得了，不用多说了，我都知道了。
   Enough! That's enough. Don't explain anymore. I know it.

77. 他们说得好好的，为什么后来会打了起来？
   They were talking civilly to each other. How did a fight begin?

78. 他这个人很会做口头人情，说得很多，不见得都做得到。
   He's that type of a person who talks a lot of generosity but seldom puts what he says into action.

79. 说吧，还不是时候，不说吧，出了事可怎么得了？
   It's not the right time to say it. But if I don't say it now, it may be too late.

80. 想不到自家人会打自家人，还打成这个样子，动都动不了。
   It's inconceivable that they fought among themselves even to the extent that they were all so badly injured that they couldn't move!

81. 他们这样面对面的，看来看去，后来，不得了，就地打了起来。
   They stared at each other for a while, and then started fighting on the spot.

82. 请你看一下，我一下子就回来。
   Can you look after this, please? I'll be right back.

C. Love

1. 多年以来，我心里只有他，他对人对事，说一不二，是个道地的好人。

   There has been only him in my heart all these years. He's a good man. He deals fairly with people and things.

2. 一年到头我心里想的只有他，现在我又发现他也是心里只有我。

   I've thought of no one but him the whole year round. And I've just discovered that he's been thinking of me too.

3. 我到这里来，是为了想见你一面。

   I came here because I wanted to see you.

4. 我一回到家，一心只想见到我的心上人，明天就要去看他。

   All I wanted was to see my sweetheart when I got home. I'm going to see him tomorrow.

5. 这几天，我老是没有见到他，他的来头不小，人的个头又好看，有时我不要想他，可他老在我心里出现。

   I've not seen him at all these few days. He comes from a good family and is very good-looking. I don't want to think about him but he's always in my mind.

6. 他这个人，我从小到大，也明了个一二，他是说什么也不会有二心的。

   I've watched him grow up so I know him well. He won't cheat on you.

7. 他会心地看一看我，说："你看天下这么大，可是你我这样要好的一对，还不多见！"

    He looked at me tenderly and said, "This is such a big world but couples as loving as us are indeed very few."

8. 他对你这么好，你就和他一起走好了。

    Since he treats you so well, you might as well go steady with him.

9. 打从那一天起，他们二人就成了一对情人了。

    Ever since that day, they have become lovers.

10. 我从来没和他分开过，这还是头一回，不知怎么好。

    I've never been separated from him. This is the first time. I don't know what to do.

11. 不要回想过去的事了，那时候我们成天在一起，一起吃，一起做事，就和自家人一个样。

    Let bygones be bygones. Then we ate and worked together, as if we were family. But those days are gone now.

12. 这样好看的人，人人都会一看就中。

    He's such a good-looking person. He commands everyone's attention.

13. 他这个人，一下子对我好，一下子对我不好，这几天我心里老是七上八下地不自在。

    He's so erratic towards me. Sometimes he's so warm. At other times he's so cool. I've been feeling very uneasy for the past few days.

14. 他有什么好，你对他这么多情？

    Why are you so emotionally attached to him? What do you see in him?

15. 你和他，一来二去的，不出一年，就成一对小情人了。

    The two of you must have got to know each other very well because in less than a year you've become young lovers.

16. 你也老大不小了，是成家的时候了，你有没有想过："他是个老好人，对你又是从不二心的。你可不要小看人，你见过那么多人，不是个个都是这样的，对不对？"

    You're no more a child. You're of marriageable age. Have you ever thought that he's a good man and is faithful to you? Don't despise him. You've met all sorts of people. Are there many like him around?

17. 他这样看得起你，你还不动心，那可就说不过去了。

    He thinks so highly of you, and yet you're not moved. That's hard to fathom.

18. 他这个人，好是很好，可是从来就没打动过我的心。

    He's a nice person indeed, but he has never come close to my heart.

19. 他是那么多情的一个人，可是还是打不动我的心。

    He's a very affectionate person but he doesn't interest me at all.

20. 他看中一个不三不四的人，出走有好几天了，家里的人一心要他回头，可是到现在也不见他回来。

He took a fancy to a person of dubious character and left with her. The entire family is awaiting his return. But until now there is no sign of it.

21. 看中看不中，都是你自己一个人的事，去好好想一想。

Whether you like him or not is your personal affair. Think it over carefully.

22. 只要他回心就好了，过去的事不在我心上。

As long as he'll come back to me, I won't hold the past against him.

23. 你想和他要好，我看这事十有八九是不成的。

You want to befriend him? I think it'll be quite difficult.

24. 他们二人老在一起，人家会不会说什么？

Both of them always stick together. People will talk, no doubt.

25. 只要我们"二人一心"，多大的事也会经得起。

If we're of one mind, we can stand up to any challenge.

D. Advice

1. 你要学好，要上进，用心做人，知不知道？
    You must learn to behave, to improve yourself and to get along with people. Do you understand?

2. 从小不学好，大了不会有成就！
    If you never learnt what's right from young, how can you be a successful person when you grow up?

3. 要小心做人，多学学他老人家。
    If you want to be an upright person, you must learn from the old man.

4. 你大了，也学你老子一样开车，好不好？
    When you grow up, you should follow your father's footsteps and learn how to drive.

5. 做事小心过头也不好，什么也做不成。
    Being overly cautious isn't good either. Nothing will come from it.

6. 你要走，也好，到了那里，自己要小心。这里有老二在，不会出什么事的。
    Go if you must. And do take care of yourself when you get there. Don't worry about things here. There's Second Brother to look after us.

7. 他是个心口不一的人，你为他做事，可得小心。
    He's a man who never keeps his promises. You've to be extra careful if you're working for him.

8. 我的天，这样不人道的事，可是你做的？
   My God, did you do such an inhuman thing?

9. 他是个大有成就的人，你以后要学他。
   He's a very successful man. You should learn from him.

10. 这事主要还在你自己，做得来，就去做；做不来，也没什么大不了。做人要自己想得开。
    This matter rests entirely on yourself. If you can do it, do it. If you can't then don't feel bad about it. You mustn't be too hard on yourself.

11. 这个人看起来不是好人，你还是走开的好。
    This person looks suspicious. You'd better keep away.

12. 他很有见地，有一天我要你去见他。
    He's very sharp. I must take you to see him one day.

13. 你不用多心，我不是在说你。
    Don't be suspicious. I'm not talking about you.

14. 你成天不开心，要不要出去走走？
    You've been unhappy the whole day. Shall we go for a walk?

15. 看你不三不四的样子，大了也不见得会出人头地。
    Just take a look at yourself. I just don't see how you'll grow up to be anyone outstanding.

16. 这事不用你说，人人都会做。
    We don't need your advice. We know what to do.

17. 有事就说吧，我们都是自己人，不会怎么样的。

If there is any problem, speak up. We're all family. It's no big deal.

18. 自大的人，从来就是不得人心的。

The proud have no supporters.

19. 说是说，做是做，事情还是一样要进行的。

No matter what you say or do, the matter has to proceed as originally planned.

20. 做人不可以有成见，有了成见，什么也学不成。

One should not be prejudiced. If one is, he'll never succeed in learning anything.

21. 只要面对自己，还有什么做不成的？

As long as you're true to yourself, what is there that you can't do?

22. 一个人要是没有主见，就不用想出人头地了。

If one has no opinion, one can never hope to succeed.

23. 不要老以为自己了不起，人家可不是这样看的。

Don't always think the world of yourself. Others may not see it that way.

24. 不要过多用心在小事情上头。

Don't waste time on trivial matters.

25. 有人说"成事在天"，又说"事在人为"，做人，还是要做事，要做有用的人。

There is a saying that goes "success depends on heaven", yet another says "success depends on one's own efforts". I think that we, as human beings, have to work in order to be useful.

26. 现在都什么时候了，你还有这样的成见？

How prejudiced you are! Which era do you think we are in now?

27. 到你老年的时候，不要为了自己几十年只吃不做来不开心。

When you're old, don't regret what you didn't do when young.

28. 你要好好地回想一下，这事情的前后经过，有什么不对，有什么不好，自己心里知道了。

Think over carefully the sequence of events: what went wrong and what was bad. You'll understand it by and by.

29. 你有事可以和他说，他这个人很会出点子，会为你想出很多点子的。

If you've got problems, talk to him. He has a lot of ideas and will help you think of the answers to your questions.

30. 我看这样做也不见得好得了多少，人前人后，你就少说点吧，行不行？

The way I see it, doing it your way won't necessarily be of any use. May be it's better that you don't push your views, all right?

31. 怎么说？这可开不了头，你从前面进来，他打后面出去，我说什么也不好。

What can I say? It's difficult for me to bring up this matter. Both of you refuse to see each other. Whatever I say won't be helpful.

32. 要是你说不动他，我也不知道说什么好。

If you can't convince him, I wouldn't know what to say to him.

33. 你要怎么样就怎么样吧。我已经说了好多了，你自己去想一想吧。

You do as you think fit. I've said a lot already. You'll have to think it out yourself.

34. 你怎么这么想不开？事情没什么大不了的。

Why can't you resolve it? The matter isn't so serious.

35. 你心里想什么，就说出来，好不好？

Tell me what's in your mind.

36. 那得看你自己怎么想，人家说什么也没有用。

It all depends on what you think. What other people say doesn't really matter.

37. 我看这事不对头，不可以这样做下去。

I think there is something wrong. We can't carry on like this.

38. 人到老年，心情还是天天那么好。

When one gets to old age, he can still be in high spirits.

39. 他那样的小人，他说什么，你也知道。

He's a mean character. You know what he says.

40. 这样自动自发的人我还没见过，人家还没开学，他就都做好了。可见事在人为，一个人中用不中用，主要还是看自己。

I haven't met a person so full of initiative. Even before the school term begins he's completed his assignments. This is self-motivation.

41. 他这个人一不好吃，二不好事，一家大小的家用，都是他出，看来他是个不可多得的人。

He's not greedy and he doesn't make trouble. He supports the whole family. There're few like him around.

42. 他一来好动，二来好事，看来不会有什么大用。

He's restless person and a trouble-maker. I don't think much good will come from him.

43. 他这个人老是和人过不去，这样下去，自己也不开心。

He can't get along with anyone. I don't think he can ever be happy.

44. 他为人很老成，可以经得起大事。

He's a matured person; he'll be able to shoulder responsibilities.

45. 他那个不三不四的样子，我看了心里很不自在。

His behaviour is horrible. I feel so uneasy about it.

46. 你说得都对，可是我做不到。

You're right. I just can't do it.

47. 你几时上我家来？我家里有很多小说，要不要过来看看？

When are you coming to my place? I have a lot of novels. Come and have a look.

48. 我会是会，不过只会一点，还做得不好。

I have a little knowledge on this but not enough to enable me to do a good job.

E. Family

1. 有这样的一家人，老头子动不动就打人，家人都不要和他在一起，到头来他只得一个人过，后来有一天，老头子不在了，大家都很开心。

There is a family where the old man often beats up his household. The family members avoided him like the plague. After he died, everyone was happy.

2. 明后天他老人家就回来了，你还是好好和他说说，没什么大不了的事。

He'll return either tomorrow or the day after. Talk to him about this nicely. It's only a small matter.

3. 我家老头，大前年就不在了，家里现在只有我一人做主。

My father passed away three years ago. I'm the head of the household now.

4. 以前我家里就老头一人在家，现在大家都回来了。

Formerly there was only my father in the house. Now all of us have come home.

5. 经过了那么多年，一家人还得以会面，那可是说不上有多开心了！
After so many years, it's really a joy to have this family reunion.

6. 一说起家用，一个个都起来走开去了。
When we got to talking about the household expenditure, everyone started to get up and walk away.

7. 那小子可不是没大没小的？他老子说他，他还老还口。
Isn't that child extremely disrespectful? He always answers back at his father.

8. 你怎么看起来，不大对头，家里出了什么事吧？
You don't look good. Did something happen at home?

9. 他们一家大小五口，都在为地主做工。
The whole family of five work for the landlord.

10. 看明天会不会是个好天，一家大小走三四里地过去看看他老人家。
If tomorrow is a fine day, we should all take a walk out to see Grandpa.

11. 大前年年成好的时候，我一家五口还有得吃，现在三个小的都大了，我们也老了，可是一天还吃不上一口面，这年头可没得过了。
Times were still good three years ago. There was more than enough to eat for the family. The children are all grown now but times are bad. There's hardly enough to eat.

12. 这是这么一回事：打从他家老头前年去了，我们就不到他家去。

Ever since his father passed away the year before, we haven't visited his family.

13. 他们是那个老头的后人，有什么事，你对他们说好了。

They're the old man's descendants. If you have any questions speak to them.

14. 他出家都有三年了，可是他家人还成天成年地想他。

Although it's three years since he left home to be a monk, his family still thinks of him.

15. 他在这里很吃得开，你来看看也好，看看他自己的小天地。

He's well sought after. Come and see him. See the world he's created for himself.

16. 他有他自己的小天地，成天开心得很。

He lives in his own small world. He's happy every day.

17. 他天天做家事，做得又多又好。

He does a lot of household chores every day. He's really good at them.

18. 你看他就这么几下子，家事就做好了，做得还很有样子。

He managed to complete all his domestic jobs with little effort.

19. "你吃过没有？"
    "还没有。"
    "来，我们一起吃！我也还没有。"
    "Have you eaten?"
    "No, I haven't."
    "Come, let's eat. I haven't eaten either."

20. "看车，看车，你成天只会看车。那是进口车，我说过，不是我们家出得起的，你要车，你自己出好了。"
    "You spend the whole day looking at cars. That car you want is an imported model. I've already told you that we can't afford it. If you want it, get it yourself."

21. 那是进口车，我是看中了，就是出不起，到头来也不得不想开了。
    That's an imported car. I do want it, but I can't afford it. Well, I've to learn not to take things too much to heart.

22. 事情怎么都成的。你要我去，我就去，你不要我去，我就在这里。你看怎么样？
    It doesn't matter one way or the other. If you want me to go, I'll go. If you want me to stay, I'll stay. What shall it be?

23. 他说是说得头头是道，可是做起来就不是那么回事。
    When you hear him talk about it, it seems clear and logical. But he doesn't carry out what he says.

24. 这事不只我这么说，他也这么说。
    He shares my feelings regarding this matter.

25. 这事可大可小，就看你要这样做，还是那样做。

This matter can both be considered a small matter and a serious one. It all depends on what you do.

26. 你说说这事情的前后经过好不好？大家也可以好好想一想。

How about telling us how it all happened? Then we can think it over properly.

27. 那事情的前后经过，他都一五一十地和我说明了。

He's told me everything about the matter.

28. 这事没有什么大不了，大家一起来做，一下子就成了。

It's only a small task. If everybody lends a hand, it'll be finished in no time.

29. 这人在这里，什么事也做不成，开年我想打发他回去了。

He can't do anything. At the beginning of next year, I'm going to send him back.

30. 他不是不会做，是成心不要做。

It is not that he's unable to do the job; he's just unwilling to do it.

31. 事情不多，我一个人做得来。

There aren't many things to do. I can handle them by myself.

32. 事情还是说开的好，一经说开，人们就都知道了。

It's better to talk things openly. Everyone will get a clear picture then.

33. 这事只要你开口，你一开口，没有不成的。
This matter depends on you. If only you'd talk about it, then it can be settled.

34. 你要是不出面，大会就开不成了。
If you don't convene it, the meeting will never come about.

F. Work

1. 这里有工事在进行中，车子不可以从这里经过。
Road works are in progress. Cars aren't allowed to pass through.

2. 这个工地的工人，大多是去年进来的，上工还不到一年。
Most of the workers at this worksite came only last year. They've been on the job for less than a year.

3. 工事进行得还可以，到明年的这个时候，就可以做成了。
The construction work is progressing well. By this time next year, it should be completed.

4. 工地这就开工了，只见工人们三三五五地都走进来了。
Work has begun on the worksite. The workers have been streaming in threes and fives.

5. 明天开会的地点在工地进口那里，主要是看看大家怎样分工。
The venue for tomorrow's meeting is the entrance to the worksite. We shall be discussing the distribution of work.

6. 这工地三年前动工到现在还没做成。

Work started three years ago. Until now it has still not been completed.

7. 他回家以后，这样想也不是，那样想也不是，后来还是回到工地来了。

He went back home to think things through. Finally, he decided to return to the worksite.

8. 工人里面就是他个子大，可是他中看不中用，什么事也做不来。

Among the workers, he's the biggest. But looks are deceiving; he can't do anything.

9. 小说一开头就这样说："这一天，打从天明以后，工地的进口那里，就有好多工会的头子和大小工人进进出出，来来去去地走。"

The novel begins thus: "On this day, since daybreak, the worksite saw many union leaders and workers going in and out."

10. 他在工会做事也有七八年了，对工人就学的事很有心得，他会做好这事的。

He's been working in the union for seven or eight years and has a lot of experience in conducting courses for the workers. He can do this job.

11. 三天以后，他和工会的头子在工地会面，发现还有很多事是去年在大会上说过的，经过了一年还没做成。

After three days he met up with the union leaders at the worksite. He discovered then that many matters which had been agreed upon at previous year's annual meeting had not been carried out.

12. "…以上的事，是我们去年已经做过了的；以下的事，是我们明年就要做的…"
The above items were done last year. The items following are those which we have to do next year.

13. 明天开工了，工人有老的，也有小的。
Work starts tomorrow. The workers comprise old ones and young ones.

14. 这个工地，去年工人做的工时，大大多过前年。
The workers working at this worksite last year worked very much longer than those the year before.

15. 车子开到工地，大家都下车了，只有那老头一人还在车上。
Upon arrival at the worksite, everybody alighted from the car. Only the old man remained in the car.

16. 有一个老头子，从工地那头走了过来。
There is an old man coming from the worksite.

17. 他家就在工地对面，一走就到。
His house is opposite the worksite. It's just a few minutes' walking from here.

18. 去吧，又没车子；不去吧，又要开会。
We don't have a car to take us there but our presence is needed at the meeting.

19. 你自己明明对我说过要开会，为什么还要出去？
You told me you were going to attend the meeting. Why are you going out instead?

20. 他从事这一行，已经有三十年以上的心得了。

He has over thirty years' experience in this profession.

21. 我看，这事要么你去，要么我去，你去想想看。

You'd better decide whether it's to be you or me who is going.

22. 还是你去好了，你对那里的国情知道得多，是不是？

Since you know a lot about the country, it's better for you to go.

23. 这事看来是可以做的，你想是不是？

We can do it. Don't you think so?

24. 你走吧！这里的事，我来做。

You may go now. I'll take charge of things here.

25. 他是个小个子，这事不见得是他做得来的。

He's of such small build. He mightn't be able to do the job.

26. 他在地里，前前后后，来来去去地看也看不到一个人。

He wandered around the field and looked back and forth. Not a person was in sight.

27. 三年来，他什么都不做，什么都不想，一心只想出国。

For the past three years, all he's done is think about how to get abroad.

28. 我一时想不起来事前他是个什么样子，事后有人说，他出车的时候，看起来还好好的，后来不知道几时出了事，就成了这个样子了。

I can't recall how he looked before. When he drove his car to work, he looked all right. I don't know what happened during the accident which made him look different.

29. 他们二人说好，要是事情做得成，得到什么，二人对开，一人五成，就这样，说一不二，说到做到。

They had agreed that if the attempt was successful, they would share what they gained equally. Each one would get 50% share.

30. 你看，这里是进口，那里是出口；也就是说，车子只可以从这里进去，从那里出来。开车的时候要小心，知道吗？

This is the entrance and that is the exit. In other words, a car can only enter here and go out from there. Be careful when you drive, won't you?

G. Study

1. 好开心，好开心！明年我可以进大学了！
Isn't it marvelous? I can go to university next year!

2. 开学了，老大和老二都天天去上学，家里只有老三。老三还小，一个人在家没事做，也想有一天可以去上学。

School term has started. The eldest and the second child will be attending classes every day. The third child will be at home. He's still very young. He has nothing to do at home except to wait for his turn to go to school.

213

3. 明天开学了，你家老二要不要和我们一起开车去上学？

The school term will start tomorrow. Will your second child be going with us in our car to school?

4. 老大上小学，今年学得好，一家老小，上上下下，都为他开心。

The eldest among us is in primary school. He did well this year. Everyone in the family is happy for him.

5. 我们从小学起，就天天一道上学。二人成为知己，少说也有十几二十年了。

We've been going to school together ever since our primary school days. We've been close friends for more than twenty years.

6. 他老人家只上过小学，他的国学那么好，都是他自学来的。

The old man has only gone through primary school education. Yet his Mandarin and understanding of Chinese culture is very good. This is all through self-study.

7. 他都二十几岁了，可是还在上中学！

He's already in his twenties but is still in high school.

8. 他上中学的时候，样样走在头里，做事用心得很。

During his high school days, he always topped the class. He worked very hard.

9. 他是大学时事学会的发起人，去年一年开过十回大会。

He was the founder of the "Current Affairs Society" in the university. There were ten general meetings last year.

10. 大学里时事学会那天开会的时候，到会的人还不到二十个。

When the university's "Current Affairs Society" had a meeting that day, the attendance was very poor. There were no more than twenty persons.

11. 在大学里，他的学说从来就是自成一家的。

At the university, his theory is considered a unique one.

12. 他是好样的，人人都以为他的学说很有见地。

He sets a good example. Everyone thinks his theory is sound.

13. 你可不可以说说中国道家学说的要点？

Are you able to explain the main principles of the Taoist doctrine?

14. "知之为知之，不知为不知，是知也。"

If you know, you know. If you don't, you won't. This is how it goes.

15. 只要你用心学，没有什么是学不会的。

As long as you try your best to learn, nothing can stop you from acquiring the know-how.

16. 他样样都会，学什么都是一学就会，可了不起了。

He's a man of many talents and a fast learner. He's truly outstanding.

17. 他还小过我，现在上大学都三年了。可见一
    个人上进还是不上进，主要还是看自己。
    He's younger than I, and he's already in the third year of his
    university course. It's obvious that one must depend on
    oneself for further advancement.

18. 我来到这里，什么都得从头学起，要不，人
    家会看不起的。
    I'm here to learn from scratch, otherwise, people will look
    down on me.

19. 这样有用的学说，你为什么不学一学？
    It's such a useful theory. Why don't you study it?

20. 这年头会做对子的人不多了，你会不会？
    There are very few people who can write antithetical
    couplets. Do you know how to compose them?

21. 大家都说那小说好看，我看过了，头三面还
    过得去，后面的就没有什么看头了。
    Everyone agreed that this novel was interesting. I found that
    the first three pages readable but not the rest of the book.

22. 你有没有想过要出国？出去走走看看，可以
    一面看一面学。
    Have you ever thought about going abroad? You'll learn
    and see new things.

23. 你学车三年了，现在会不会开车？
    You've already been learning to drive for the last three
    years. Are you able to drive now?

24. 这事什么人做都一样，你也可以和他做得一样好。

Anybody can do the job. You can also do the job as well as him.

25. 我还没见过他这样有上进心的人。

I've never met such a self-motivated person.

26. 对不起，我年少无知，学了三年，还是一事无成。

I'm young and ignorant. After three years of study, I haven't accomplished anything.

H. Society

1. 中国的四大发明，天下没有一个人不说好。

Chinese's four great inventions are acclaimed worldwide.

2. 中国的国情现在开明多了，自从一九八一年以来，年成大大地好起来，出国的人一年多过一年，人们过得也一年好过一年，国家大事有人大开会做主。

China is now more open to the outside world. Since 1981 harvests have increased, more people are going abroad and the standard of living is improving. Important national issues are now decided by the People's Congress.

3. 前几年中国的年成好，在我老家，人人要什么，有什么，这可好了。

A few years back, China had a bumper harvest. In my home town, everyone had enough and more. Wasn't that good?

4. 在你们老家那里，人们过得好不好？
Do people in your home town lead comfortable lives?

5. 自从过年以来，在我们老家那里，好人好事可多得很。
Since the new year kind people and good deeds have been springing up everywhere in my home town.

6. 在中国，现在上上下下人人都想出国，这是什么一回事，你可不可以说明一下？
Please explain why everyone in China wants to go abroad.

7. 上回一九八六年的那个大会，中国是发起国。
China was the host nation of the 1986 Conference.

8. 打那年"九一八起"，国人都知道了中国的对头是什么人。
Since the September 18th Incident, the Chinese know who their real enemies are.

9. 这个国家还没有开发，以后可做的事情，还多得吧。
This country has yet to be developed. There is a lot of potential for the future.

10. 这个国家的国都在这里，这是个大都会，在大都会的中心，人口多，车子也多。
This is the capital. It's a big city crowded with people and vehicles.

11. 这个国家的人很会学人家，人家的车头，他
学，人家的工会，他也学。
This country's good at imitating the products of others.
From car engines to concepts like trade unionism, they're
prepared to put their hands to them.

12. 事情是这样的：去年五国大会在中国开会的
时候，有的国家要多出口自己的车子；有的
国家又不要进口过时的车子。有的国家很看
不起那一国的工人；那一国又很看不起这一
国的发明家。后来有中人出面说和和，就是
不要大家口头上说来说去，还是要多多开发
自己的国家。
It's like this: at the five-nation conference last year in
China, some countries wanted to export more of their
vehicles while others were against the importing of obsolete
models. Yet others looked down on the productivity and
inventions of certain countries. In the end after a country
came forward to play the mediatory role, all the countries
decided not to deliberate further but instead to continue to
develop their own countries in their own ways.

13. 为了要为国家多做出口起见，人们上下一
心，一面有工会来发动工人，一面又起用好
多小工来做人发，想不到做成以后，是那么
的好看。后来这上好的人工头发就成为国家
的主要出口了。
To improve the country's exports the people decided to
work together in the manufacture of wigs. The unions so
motivated the workers that their products were of excellent
quality. In the end wigs became the country's main export.

14. 这是进口车，在这里很吃得开。
This is an imported car. It's very popular here.

15. 这是什么国家出的车子，这么不经用！三天五天地出事，可不中用了！

This is a lousy car. Where is it from? It breaks down every few days; it's really useless.

16. 在大都会里，车有车行道，人有人行道，就是自行车也有自行车道。

In a big city traffic is very orderly. Motor vehicles have designated motorways, pedestrians have pedestrian walkways and bicycles have bicycle tracks.

17. 现在大国也好，小国也好，都自个自主，看样子，天下不会有不得了的大事了。

These days small and big countries alike have their own individual sovereignity. Seems like there is nothing too big that it can't be solved.

18. 中国的事只要一经人大开会，事情就可以做成了。

The People's Congress is the policy-making body of China. If it passes a proposal it'll be followed through.

19. 出国走动了一年，到头来还是自己的老家好。

After being abroad for one year, I feel that home is still the best place.

20. 自从几年前和会开过后，就从来没有打来打去的事了。

Ever since the peace conference a few years ago, there hasn't been anymore fighting.

21. 这是国会的车，什么人也不得动用。

This car belongs to Parliament. Nobody can use it.

22. 他这个人天天想的只有国家大事，以国事为中心。

All he thinks about are the affairs of the state. The country is his centre of focus.

23. 年年过年都有人过不去，不过现在过得去的人，一年会多过一年。

Many people find that they're unable to balance their accounts at the end of the year. But things are improving now. There are now more people who can better manage their own finances.

24. 年成不好，你还大吃大用的，这不是自己和自己过不去？

We're all in a recession and you're still overspending. You're at odds with yourself, aren't you?

25. 要是他在国会开会的时候，不主动地说"对不起"，以后就会出事的。

Things will get unpleasant if he doesn't apologize at the parliamentary session.

23. Dialogues

(1)

A : 我想明天去看你，行不行？

B : 对不起，明天我有事，后天吧！怎么样？

A : 好的，后天我去。

B : 你怎么来？是不是自己开车？

A : 是的。你要我几点去？

B : 三点，你看好不好？

A : 好的，那么我们就后天三点见面吧！多时不见，我有好多事要和你说说。

对不起，明天我有事，后天吧！

A : I'm thinking of visiting you tomorrow if that's all right with you.

B : I'm very sorry but I'll be busy tomorrow. What about the day after?

A : All right, I'll be there the day after.

B : How will you come? Will you be driving?

A : Yes. What time would you like me to go?

B : Three o'clock if it suits you.

A : That's fine. I shall see you the day after tomorrow at three o'clock then. It's been a long time since we last met, and there are quite a few things I'd like to talk to you about.

(2)

A : 为 (wéi) 人不可多情，你说对不对？

B : 那要看你怎么做，有的时候也不见得不好。

A : 你不知道，我家老大就是十分多情，见一个，要一个。到现在少说也有过十几个了，一个也没成。

B : 什么？还没成家？

A : 可不是？四十大几的人了，还成天不三不四的，不成个样子！

B : 你不是不知道，现在的人，都不要成家，和我们那时候不一样了。

A : 看样子，我们都过时了。过了时的人，还是少说一点的好！

少说也有过十几个了，一个也没成。

A : Men should not be too flirtatious, don't you agree?

B : It really depends, in some cases it's not entirely bad.

A : I'm thinking of my eldest son, who flirts outrageously. He's always chasing girls. I would say that he's had more than ten girlfriends already and yet he's still not married.

B : What? He's still not married?

A : Absolutely. He's already in his late forties, and yet he's behaving irresponsibly.

B : Don't you know, nowadays people do not want to get married, unlike our time.

A : Looks like we're the old-fashioned ones. And it's better that we "oldies" keep quiet then.

(3)

A：　怎么了？有什么事？

B：　没什么，车子开得不对，得 (děi) 从前面走。

A：　前面只有一个进口，要是你不小心看，一下子就走
　　　过了，走过了，要走回头，可就没那么好走了。

B：　我知道，我会小心看。

A：　说是这么说，可是做起来，就不是那么一回事了。

B：　我们走走看吧，事情没做过是不知道的。

怎么了？有什么事？

A：　What's happened? What's the matter?

B：　I took the wrong way; I should have entered by the
front.

A：　The front has only one entrance, and if you're
not careful you could easily miss it. Once you've

missed it, it would be quite difficult to make a
turn back.

B : I know. I'll be careful to look out for it.

A : It's easier said than done.

B : Let's give it a try. You'll never know until you have
tried.

(4)

A : 国会明天要开会了。

B : 你知道不知道要开几小时？

A : 我想得开三小时。

B : 你会不会去？

A : 会的，我会去。

B : 那么，我也去。

A : 好，我们明天见。

B : 明天见。

好，我们明天见。

A : The parliamentary meeting will open tomorrow.

B : Do you know how many hours will it take?

A : I think it would take three hours.

B : Will you be going?

A : Yes, I will certainly go.

B : In that case, I'll come along.

A : Good. We'll meet tomorrow.

B : Tomorrow then.

(5)

A : 这是我从前的中学，你过来看看。

B : 什么？是你的中学？我从前也是在这里。

A : 那可好了，这么说，我们都是自己人了。

B : 可不是？没想到你我都是来自这中学。

A : 那是几年前的事？

B : 我想想，好多年了，看我都这么大了，有八年了。
对，是八年前的事了。

A : 对我来说，也有五、六年了，那还是一九八六年。

B : 你看，现在我们都是成年人了，是不是？

这是我从前的中学，你过来看看。

A : This is my former secondary school. Come and take a look.

B : Oh, was this really your school? I was also formerly from this school.

A : That's marvellous. That means we're buddies.

B : That's right. I never thought we both came from the same school.

A : How many years ago was that?

B : Let me think. It has been many years since… going by my age it should be about eight years ago. That's right, eight years have passed since I left the school.

A : In my case, I left the school five or six years ago. And that was 1986.

B : You see, we've grown up, haven't we?

(6)

A： 他很小的时候就会开车，你看，他开得多好！

B： 说的是，我看得出。他开车有几年了？

A： 我看已经有十二、三年了，从来没出过什么事。

B： 我要是也那么小心就好了。不行，我事多，开车的时候老是分心，上一回还出了事。

A： 后来怎样了？

B： 还好没什么，我才走得了 (liǎo)，你可不要对人说起这事。"心不二用"对我来说，可就做不到！

A： 不会的，有心做，就会做到！

上一回还出了事。

A : He started driving at a young age. See, how well he drives!

B : You're right, I can see that. How long has he been driving?

A : I believe it must be about 12 or 13 years now, and he's never had an accident.

B : If only I could be as careful as him! But I always have things on my mind, and when I drive, I get easily distracted. That's why I had an accident once.

A : Oh, what happened then?

B : Luckily, it wasn't serious and I got away with it. It's so embarrassing, so I'd rather not talk about it. Because I have a tendency to be distracted, I don't seem to be able to concentrate.

A : Don't be negative. If you have the will, you will succeed.

(7)

A : 几点了？你吃了没有？

B : 还没有，不过我不想吃。

A : 那怎么行？来，我们一起吃吧！

B : 我什么也吃不下。这几天事情多，去年没做好的事，都得(děi)在这个年头做好。我已经三天不想吃了。

A : 事多也得吃，对不对？我看这样吧，你就少吃一点，吃过之后，回去做事，好不好？人，不吃是不行的。

来，我们一起吃吧！

A : What time is it? Have you had your meal?

B : No, but I don't feel like eating.

A : That's not good for you. Let's have something to eat together.

B : I have no appetite. I've been awfully busy trying to finish last year's backlog that I've lost my appetite for three days already.

A : You still should have your meals, no matter how busy you are. Why don't you just eat a little now, then go back to work. You can't very well go without food.

(8)

A： 什么时候了？

B： 你是不是六点要回家？到时候我们一起走吧！你看
怎么样？

A： 好的。现在几点了？

B： 五点四十五分。多一下子，我们就走。

A： 你说什么？多一下子？我看不对吧！

B： 对！你看我这个人…。

A： 我还可以多做一点，就快做好了。

到时候我们一起走吧！

A : What time is it?

B : Would you be going home at six? By then, we can leave together if you don't mind it.

A : That's fine. What's the time now?

B : It's 5.45 p.m. We can leave in a little while.

A : Did you say 'a little while'? I think you're wrong.

B : Oh yes! Really, I must be getting…(absent minded).

A : I can still do a bit more work; it'll be finished soon.

(9)

A : 你明天几点上工？

B : 还不是一样，八点，怎么了？

A : 没什么，我以为你可以不用去了。

B : 有这么好的事就好了。

A : 那么几点回来？也一样是六点吧！

B : 我现在还不知道，得 (děi) 明天到了工地，看工头要我做什么。

A : 少做点，行 (xíng) 不行？

B : 不行，现在这个工头，是个没情面的人，人人都得多做，不只我一个。

你明天几点上工？

A : What time do you start work tomorrow?

B : At 8 a.m., as usual. What's the matter?

A : It's nothing. I thought you don't have to go to work tomorrow.

B : It would be nice if that were so!

A : So what time would you return? At 6 p.m., as usual?

B : I'm not sure. I'll know when I get to the worksite tomorrow. It depends on what my supervisor wants me to do.

A : Can't you cut down on your work?

B : Definitely not. This present supervisor is very strict and everyone, not just me, has to work harder.

(10)

A： 好了，不要走了，就在这里吧。那里有几对情人。

B： 那有什么？天下有情人多的是！来，过来一点。

A： 看你，就是要人家不开心。

B： 来，我有事要和你说。

A： 你说过好多回了。

B： 这一回不一样。

A： 好，你说吧。

B： 是不是有人对你说，不要和我好？

A： 有人说…有人说你为人不大好。

B： 这是什么人，成心和我过不去？

A： 有人说，你是个心口不一、自我中心的人。又有人说，你只看上不看下。是不是这样？

B： 是不是这样，你以后就知道了。就有这样的人，老是要说人家的不是！

A： 我看，是你自己不得人心，是不是？不过，你只要对我好就行了。

B： 我会的。你说，我是不是你的心上人？

A： 还说不上。

B： 这不是你心里想说的吧！人家说的，你想开点，自己要有主见，没什么大不了的。他们是吃多了没事做！人前人后说的都不一样，可不是"知人知面不知心"？

A： 好了，不要想这么多了。人家说人家的，我们做我们的。

B： 我也是这么说，你看我们想的都一样。只要我们在一起开心，人家说什么都是人家的事，对不对？会有那么一天他们看得见的。

来，我有事要和你说。

A : Let's stop here and not go any further. There are some lovers over there.

B : What's wrong with that? The world is full of lovers. Come closer.

A : You see, you really know how to annoy people.

B : Come on, I have something to say to you.

A : But you've already said it many times.

B : This is a different matter now.

A : All right, what is it?

B : Has somebody been telling you to break up with me?

A : According to some people...well, some people did say your conduct is rather undesirable.

B : Who are these people who insist on criticizing me?

A : Some people say you're not sincere and self-centred. Others say that you only look up to the rich and the powerful. Is that true?

B : Whether it's really true, you'll find out by and by. But there are people who are bent on picking faults with others.

A : I think you're simply unpopular with people, right? But I'll be satisfied if you'd be good to me.

B : I certainly will be good to you. Am I not your sweetheart after all?

A : I'm not so sure.

B : You're not really speaking from the heart! You shouldn't take what people tell you seriously, but form your own opinions. These people are meddlesome and anyway what they say one day may not be what they'll say the next day. Surely you know you can't judge a person by his appearance!

A : Well, all right, let's not be bothered by this. Let others say what they will, but let's get on doing our things.

B : I fully agree with you; you see, we both do think alike, after all. As long as we are happy together, what others say shouldn't affect us, right? But they'll understand us some day.

(11)

A : 你看，都一点多了。要吃点什么不？
B : 不用了，我吃过了。
A : 多吃一点吧！
B : 我已经吃了不少了。你自己来吧！
A : 那好吧。

你看，都一点多了。

A : Look, it's past one o'clock now. Shall we eat something?

B : No, thanks. I've lunched already.

A : Come on, have a bit more!

B : I've had eaten quite a lot. Just go ahead, please.

A : All right then.

(12)

A : 这几年，我是不是看起来老得多？

B : 不会！你看上去还是和以前一样，一点也不老。

A : 你不知道，这几年，我有好多不开心的事。

B : 有什么不开心的？你说说，看我是不是可以做点什么？

A : 我不想说，一时也说不了那么多。

B : 那么这样吧，有一天我去你家，我们一起开车出去走走，怎么样？

A : 那也好，在车上我会一五一十地 对你说 。

这几年，我是不是看起来老得多？

A : Do I look older in these past few years?

B : Not at all. You still look the same as before.

A : You may not be aware. I've had many unhappy experiences in the past few years.

B : What unhappy experiences? Tell me, let me see if there is anything I can do for you.

A : I don't think I want to talk about it, and in any case, I wouldn't be able to tell you all the details in such a short time.

B : All right. Why don't I pick you up at your home one day and go for a drive?

A : That'll be fine. Then I'll be able to tell you all about it.

(13)

A： 我想我得走了。
B： 为什么？
A： 我家里还有人。
B： 是不是你的老人？
A： 他还没吃，我得回去为他做点什么吃的。要是他想吃面，我就为他下点面吧！
B： 可不是？已经八点了，你去吧。

我想我得走了。

A： I think I've got to go now.
B： Why?
A： Somebody's waiting for me at home.
B： Is it your old parent?

240

A : He hasn't eaten yet. I've got to go and cook his meal. If he would like to have some noodles, I'll cook some for him.

B : You're right. It's already eight o'clock. Go home then.

(14)

A ： 来，我看看，你的头发多好看！

B ： 你的也很好。

A ： 你这么说，是要我开心吧？

B ： 到这里来，你自己看看，看见了吧！我说得对不对？

A ： 我以为还是你那样好。

B ： 我以为，这个样子对你来说，是老成了一点。

A ： 不会的，老成一点的好。

B ： 你也可以做的。

A ： 后面的，我自己做不来。

B ： 学一下，就行了，你看，这么一来，那么一去地，就好了，是不是？

你自己看看，看见了吧！

A : Come, let me have a look. Your hair style looks good!

B : Yours is nice, too.

A : Are you saying it to please me?

B : Come over here and take a look at it yourself. See! Is it what I said true?

A : I still think your style is better.

B : I think my style would look rather mature on you.

A : No. It's fine to look a little mature.

B : You can also do your hair in this style then.

A : But I wouldn't be able to do up the rear.

B : It's very easy to learn. Look, do it this way, and then that way. And it's done, isn't it?

(15)

A : 你说你会来看我的，怎么不见你来？

B : 几时？我几时说过？

A : 大前天吧，有没有？

B : 对不起，我想我没说过。

A : 好了，现在你已经来了。

B : 可不是？现在我不是在你面前了？

A : You said you would come and see me, so why was there no sign of you?

B : When? When did I ever say it?

A : About three days ago. Didn't you?

B : Sorry, I don't think I said so.

A : It's all right, as you're here.

B : That's right. Am I not right in front of you now?

(16)

A： 不知道就少开口！

B： 你怎么可以这样说？这样没大没小的？

A： 你看，这大成 对不对？

B： 怎么了？

A： 事情是这样的：大成他不知道我已经把事情做好了，就对小明说，我是个只会说不会做的人！

B： 好了，好了，很多人都是"说，是一回事：做，又是一回事"，他以为你也是这样。

A： 他不可以想什么就说什么，对不对？

B： 现在他知道了，就没事了。"只做不说"会好过"只说不做"，对不对？

A ： Keep your mouth shut if you don't know.

B ： How can you say so? With no courtesy and respect!

A ： Look, do you think Da Cheng is right?

B ： What happened?

A ： This is what happened: Da Cheng didn't know I had completed the work and told Xiao Ming that I was only a person of words without deeds!

B ： All right, all right. There are many people who are the type who would say one thing and do another. He thought you were also such a person.

A ： He shouldn't say whatever he assumes, can he?

B ： Now that he knows it, the matter should be resolved. Anyway, isn't it better to do something without saying it than to say you'll do it but not actually doing it?

(17)

A： 我这么做是不得已的，我不得不这么做！
B： 什么事？什么事？
A： 我打了他，你看，打成这样！不过我这么做是不得已的。
B： 怎么一回事？
A： 是这样的：那时候，车子开过来了，他没看见，我要是不打他，车子就会从他头上开过去，我只好行动起来，不过打得过头了，成了这样！
B： 是的，打得过头了一点，下一回可得小心！
A： 不会有"下一回"了，你看，我自己这里也开了一个大口！

我打了他，你看，打成这样！

244

A : I had no alternative but to do it. I had to do it this way!

B : What's the matter?

A : I hit him. He was really badly hurt. But I had no choice but to do it.

B : What happened?

A : It happened like this: At that time, he didn't see a car coming his way. In fact it would have knocked him on his head. I had to do something, so I hit him. But I used too much force and he ended up like this.

B : Yes, you had hit him too forcefully. You'd better be careful next time.

A : There won't be a "next time". You see, I myself got a large cut too as a result of it.

(18)

A : 他已经三天不吃不动了。

B : 怎么会这样？

A : 人老了，都会有这么一天的，你我也都一样。

B : 不过，前几天我见他还好好的。

A : 七老八十的人了，事情不好说，是不是？

B : 没什么，我想事在人为，我有开心的事，对他说一说，你看吧，他会一下子好起来！

A : 那好！现在可要看你的了！

我有开心的事，对他说一说，你看吧，他会一下子好起来！

A : He hasn't been eating and moving around for three days now.

B : Why has he become like this?

A : People do come to such a day when they grow old. The same goes for you and me.

B : But he was quite all right when I saw him several days ago.

A : Things are never certain when people are in their seventies or eighties, isn't it?

B : It's nothing serious. I think something can be done. I have some good news for him. You see, it will quickly cheer him up.

A : All right. We'll count on you now!

(19)

A：　你看见那一对情人没有？

B：　你说他们是一对？你怎么知道？

A：　不只我这么说，大成和小明也这么说。

B：　一个那么老，一个看上去只不过三十上下。你是
　　　不是以为不大对头？

A：　就是，就是。

B：　那没什么，只要他们在一起说得来，在一起过得
　　　开心，有什么不对？

A：　不过我以为，人老了，要有点自知之明，你说对不
　　　对？

B：　对是对，可是人人都不一样，是吧？。你看,有的
　　　人，少年老成；也有的人，人老心不老。他们是什
　　　么样，我们又不知道。为什么我们要说他们？

A：　说的也是，他们的事只有他们自己知道。

B：　他们都是成年人了，自己会看也会想，对自己的事，
　　　有自己的主见，我看不出有什么不好。

A：　人家说什么也没用，是不是？

B：　没有用说来做什么？还是不要说的好。

你看见那一对情人没有？

A : Can you see that couple?

B : Did you say they're a couple? How do you know it?

A : I'm not the only one who say that. Da Cheng and Xiao Ming think so, too.

B : One is so old, and the other looks no more than about thirty years old. You don't think they match, do you?

A : That's right. I don't.

B : That's not important. As long as they can communicate with each other and are happy together, there is nothing wrong with that.

A : But I think when people are old, they should have a sense of self-awareness. Don't you think so?

B : You're right. But people are different, aren't they? You see, some are young but mature and others are old but still young at heart. Since we don't know them, how can we criticize them?

A : You do have a point. As this matter concerns themselves, they should know what is best.

B : Both of them are grown-ups now. They can judge and think for themselves, and form their own opinions about their own matters. I can't see anything wrong with their relationship.

A : Whatever others may say doesn't matter, does it?

B : Since what we say doesn't matter to them, what's the use of talking about it? We'd better keep quiet.

(20)

A： 你看他，一年到头没有一天不是开开心心的。

B： 那多好！我也要学他那样。

A： 他有他自己的小小天地，主要的是，他以为："人人为我，我为人人。"这样他对"怎样做人、怎样做事"，都会开心。

B： 要是人人心里都这样想，天下就没事了！

A ： Look at him. There has not been a day throughout the year when he isn't happy and joyous.

B ： That's wonderful! I would like to learn to be like him.

A ： He lives in a small world of his own. Most importantly, he believes that we should do unto others what others do unto us. This is how he treats life and conduct himself, and keeps himself happy.

B ： If only everyone could think like he does, there would be no conflicts in this world anymore!

24. Passages

(1)

　　我见过他，可是在什么时候见过他，我想了又想：是大学的时候，还是中学、小学的时候？一时怎么也想不起来。

　　有一天，我又见到他了，他在前面走，我和我的家小在后面走。我们一前一后地走了一个多小时。后来，他回过头来看看我，开口说道："你是不是小明？"他见我没有说什么，又说，"十几年没见了，你还是老样子。"

　　我想了想，对了，他是那个工头，那个好心的工头，对什么人都很好的老工头。我好开心，我说："你也还是那个老样子。来，这是我的家人，你看，小的一个都这么大了。"

　　"你那时也这样，"他说，"也是这么大小。"

　　可不是？我小时候，天天上学都会经过他的家，他家里什么好吃的、好看的都少不了我的。他的家就和我的家一样。

　　现在已经过了十几年，我们面对面，又在一起了。回想小时候的事，我有说不出的心情。他看出我的心事，他说："来吧，来看我吧，你什么时候来都成。"不用说，那一天，我有多开心！

I have met him before but when was it? I tried to recall: was it at the university, secondary or primary school? I simply couldn't recall it on the spur of the moment.

One day I met him again. He was walking in front of me and my family. We walked in this manner for an hour or so before he finally turned around to look at me and ask, "Are you Xiao Ming?" Getting no response from me, he said, "We haven't seen each other for more than ten years, but you still look much the same as before."

After thinking hard, I realized he is that foreman — that kind-hearted foreman, that good old foreman who treated everyone very well. Delighted, I said to him, "You haven't changed much yourself. Come on, this is my family. As you can see, the youngest has already grown so much."

"When you were his age, you were like him too," he said, "you were more or less as big as him."

"Oh, really?" I pondered. When I was a child, I used to pass by his house on my way to school everyday. He was sure to share with me what nice things he had at home, be it food or playthings. His home was just like another home to me.

After a lapse of more than ten years, we've encountered each other and are together again. Reminiscing my childhood, I found myself unable to express my deep-seated feelings about those wonderful times. He sensed my emotions and said, "Come on, come visit me, you'll be welcome anytime." Without a doubt, how wonderful that day will be!

(2)

那已经是三年前的事了，我们那时都在工会里做事。自从那时和他分开以后，就没见过面，可是这一回，想不到我们又在一起开会。

开会的地点在大学的中心，我们见了面，大家都很开心。"他看上去老多了"我心里这样想，可是口里不好说。

"怎么样，过得还好吧？事情做得怎么样？"

"三年不见了，你还是老样子。我还过得去，就是事情多了一点。"

"你一家大小可都好？有没有回去过你的老家？"

"你是说中国的老家？我大前年去过，还好，现在大家都过得好多了。"

"我想明年也要去看看，可是我事多，到时候还不知道走不走得开。"

"说什么也要去的。我们是那里来的，你说对不对？"

可不是！我的家人从中国来，到现在已经有八十年了，老的老了，小的还什么都不知道。明年，说什么明年我也要和家小们一起回去走走、看看。

It was three years ago when we worked together at the union. We have never met again ever since parted with each other. Surprisingly, we met again now at a conference.

The venue of the conference was the centre of the university. We were very happy to meet again. "He has aged a lot," I thought to myself but was careful not to mention it.

"How are you getting on? How is your job?"

"I haven't seen you for three years, and you're still looking like your old self. As for me, I'm pretty well, except that I'm too busy at work."

"How is your family? Have you been to your home town?"

"Do you mean the home town in China? I've been back a few years ago. Everyone there seems better-off nowadays!"

"I'm thinking of going there next year, but I'm so busy that I don't know if I would be able to make it there then."

"No matter what you said, you should make a trip, after all we did come from there, don't you agree?"

That's right! It has been some eighty years since we all came from China. The old ones are getting aged and the young are still too young to understand. Next year, no matter what happens, I'm determined to return with my whole family for a visit there.

(3)

我们的国家，去年出国的人，是人口的三成，也就是说，三分之一的人出过国（三个人之中，就有一个是出过国的）。

怎么会这么多？这说明了现在人人都过得好，主要是大家都有事做。不出三年，我们可以回头来看看，也就是说，到了一九九八年，出国的人还会多过这几年的。有人说，会有二分之一的人是出过国的。

在过去的十年里，出国的人，也是一年多过一年。进口的车子也大大地多过这几年的。以后我国人口会多一点，日子会过得很好。

这就说明了，我们的国家大事都做得很对，做得很好。经过三十多年的开发，我国国人，大多都是有用的人，人人都在为国家做事，也都在为自己做事。

也可以这么说，人们一来到这里，只要前后走一走，看一看，就可以知道，这是个什么样的国家：天上，地下都做得那么好；小学，中学是那么的多；老的、小的都过得那么自在。要吃，有得吃；要用，有得用；要看，有得看；要什么就有什么，那还有什么可说的？

Last year, the number of people who went abroad in our country made up of about 30% of the population. In other words one-third of the population or one in three persons has been abroad.

Why is the proportion so high? Indeed it points to our present high standard of living and, more importantly, our full employment. We can assume that in three years, that is by 1998, there would be a further increase in the number of people going abroad. Some have even predicted that by then half the population would have gone abroad.

Over the past ten years, there has been a yearly increase in the number of people going abroad. Similarly, the number of cars imported has also increased a lot more than previously. Our population may increase a little and our standard of living may improve.

This proves the fact that our country has dealt with the main problems of living efficiently. After more than thirty years of development, the majority of our people have become productive citizens. Everyone is not only able to earn a living for himself but is also able to contribute to the nation.

It can be said that any visitor to our country, at one look, can see for himself what kind of country we are. From top to bottom, everything is in good order. There are numerous primary and secondary schools; and both the young and old live a comfortable life. There's not only plenty of food and daily necessities for our daily needs, there's also plenty of entertainment if we want it. We all have whatever we need, so there's nothing to complain about at all.

(4)

从我家到他家，只不过要走一个多小时。小时候我们老在一起，他大我不多，可是他自小好学，什么都要学，我见到他的时候，他都在学，时时学，天天学。我想，有一天，他会有很大的成就的。

我就不是这样，有一天，过一天，什么也不做。后来我们都大了，他成为大学里一个主要的学人，我那时还在中学。有一回他看到我，见我做人做事还没什么主见的样子，他对我说："做人，就要做个有用的人，怎样可以做个有用的人？那就要多看、多学、多想、多用。"

　　见我没说什么，他又说："只是看，那不行，还得学，好好地学，用心地学。看了，学了，还不行，那就得想：'为什么会是这样的？为什么会是那样的？'看了，学了，想了，还是不行，那就得用，多多地用，学过的都要用一用，看看是不是都对，都用得上！不是有人说过：'学到老，还学不了'，是不是？"

　　我没说什么，不过心里在想："我知是知道的，这不是人人都做得到的，我就做不到。"我一面想，一面口吃地说："是的，是的。"

　　后来，我一点一点地学，我做到了。

It takes a little more than an hour to go from my place to his house. When we were kids we were always hanging out together. He is slightly older than me, but he was very keen to learn. He was always learning about anything. Everytime I came across him, he would be studying. He did that every day. So I assumed that he would achieve something great one day.

Unlike him, I would just kill my time every day without doing anything. When we grew up, he became an important scholar at the university, whereas I was still in secondary school. Once when I met him again, noting that I did not have a definite view of life, he said to me, "You must try to be a useful person. How can you be one? One way is to see more, learn more, think more and apply more."

Getting no response from me, he pursued, "Seeing alone is useless, you must learn and learn hard. It is not enough to see and learn, you still have to think. Why is this so? Why should it be so? Even then, it is not enough to see, learn and think, you must be able to apply yourself as far as you can. You must apply whatever you have learned, test it and see if it is true, if it is applicable. Didn't someone once say, 'You learn as you grow, and there's no end to learning?"

I didn't utter a word, but thought to myself, "I do understand what you are saying, but it is not something that everyone is capable of, least of all me." Thinking thus, I stuttered, "Yes, yes."

Since then, step by step I began to learn, and I found that I could finally make it too.

(5)

我不开心已经好几天了，这是我自己心头上的事：我的自行车不见了。

我的自行车，你是知道的，我天天用，上学用，上工用，回家也用，一天也少不了。我那么小心地用，有时这里不好走，我就打从那里走。那头进不去，我就回过来从这头进。你看，现在不见了，我的心情，你是可以想见的。

我们工地那里，天天都有那么多的自行车，不知道会不会有人用了我的自行车？要是你知道，可不可以对我说说？

从前我在中国上大学的时候，学会了用自行车。你知道中国是一个以自行车为主的国家，在那里三个人之中就有一个是有自行车的。我们大学那里，前前后后看过去都是自行车，人要从那里经过，还得十分小心地走。

那时候，要是不会自行车是不行的。后来我回来这里，就多时没用了。没想到现在我在这个工地，就得用自行车了，你知道，工地这么大，走来走去都得用自行车。

在这里，你就是我的知己，我的心事你会明了，可不可以为我出个什么点子？

I've been unhappy for the past few days because of something I've kept to myself: my bicycle is lost.

As you are aware, I used my bicycle every day — to go to school, to go to work and to return home. I couldn't go without it even for a day. I used it with care; if the road was not in good condition, I would take another route. So, now that the bicycle has disappeared, you can imagine how I feel.

There are so many bicycles around in the worksite every day. I wondered if someone had taken mine. If you happen to know about it, will you please inform me?

I learned to ride the bicycle when I studied at the university in China. As you know, China is a nation which uses bicycles as a main form of transport; one in three owns a bicycle. When you look out from the university, there are bicycles everywhere, and you have to be extra cautious when passing through.

At that time, it wouldn't do if you didn't know how to ride a bicycle. Later when I returned here, I didn't use it for a long time. Unexpectedly I now have to use the bicycle at this worksite. As you know, the worksite is so huge that you would need a bicycle to get around it.

You're my closest friend here. If you can understand my feelings, could you please give me some advice?

(6)

　从前有一年要过年的时候,有个地主对他的三个工头说:"我要出国去了,我要去十天,这十天里,你们要为我看家,还有那几十个工人,行不行?"

　三个工头都说:"那还用说?我们会的。"地主走了以后,三个工头在一起开会。一个说:"太好了,明天我可以回家了。"他说走就走。

　大工头对二工头说:"我看这样吧,这八十个工人,我们来分一分,四十个老的和你一起做,四十个小的和我一起做。你看怎么样?"

　"这是怎么说?老的是你的,我要小的!"

　"你看不见?小的吃得多,又不会做!"

　"那你为什么要小的?你只是为了自己,还以为人家不知道!没这么好的事!"

　他们说来说去,后来不只动口,还打了起来。打来打去,打得二人头上都开了一个大口。那八十个工人,这时候,也都一个个地走了。

　十天以后,地主回来了,他自己走一走,家里地里,这里那里,什么人也看不见,工头也不见了。后来有人对他说:"不用看了,大家都回去过年了,过年的时候,怎么会有人做工?"

　There was once a landlord who said to his three foremen when new year was drawing near, "I'm going abroad for ten days. During this period, would you help me look after my house and scores of workers?"

The three foremen said, "Do you need to tell us that? We'll certainly do so." They held a meeting after the landlord had gone. One said, "How wonderful! I can go home tomorrow." Then he left.

The head foreman then said to the second foreman, "I think this is what we should do: Let's divide the eighty workers between us. The forty older workers will work with you and the forty younger ones will work with me. What do you think of this?"

"Why should it be as you said? You should have the older ones; I want the younger ones!"

"Don't you see? The younger ones eat a lot more food but can't do any work."

"Since this is so, why do you still want the younger ones? Don't you think that I don't know you are only being selfish. I won't be so easily tricked!"

Words were exchanged but soon after a fight broke out between them, and both injured their head. Meanwhile one by one, all the eighty workers left quietly.

Ten days passed and the landlord returned. He went around the house and the fields; and everywhere he went he didn't see a single worker neither did he see any of his foremen. Someone then said to him, "You don't have to look for them. They have all gone home for the new year celebration; who would want to work over the new year!"

(7)

打从一九九二年年头起，国会开会的时候，就在说工会的事。

以前，十八以下的工人，都不得进工会。那是他们还小，没什么主见，对什么人是好人，什么人不是好人，还分不出。什么事是对的，什么事是不对的，也还看不明。

现在可不是这样了，一来是工人已能自动、自发、自己做主；二来我们的国情也和从前大不一样了。现在工人只要到十六，就可以进工会了。

在一九九二年，五月二十日那一天，一天之中，就有四千个工人进工会。这是从来没有过的大事情。

"工会为你"，"这是你的工会"，"工会为工人，工人为工会"。工人们都很明了这点，他们说："工会就是我们的中心，走在我们的前头。工会要我们做什么，我们就做什么。"

我们也可以主动地说出一己之见，只要是为大家好。我们是工会的主人，自己的事自己做，大家的事大家想。我们都是一家人，为工会做事，就是为自己做事！

The trade union issue was discussed in Parliament when it came into session in the beginning of 1992.

Formerly workers below the age of 18 were not allowed to join the union. This is because they were considered to be immature, without a view or stand of their own, and unable to tell right from wrong.

But things are different nowadays. First, workers are able to take initiative and make decisions for themselves. Secondly, the conditions have changed in our country, making it possible for workers who are 16 years of age to join the union.

On 20 May 1992, 4,000 workers joined the union. Such a thing had never happened before.

"The union is for you", "This is your union", and "The union is for the workers, and the workers are for the union". These are slogans that our workers understand very well. This is why they said, "The union gives us focus and leads us. We'll do what it tells us to do."

All of us are allowed to use our initiative to express our individual opinion, as long as it is for the good of everybody. We are our union's own masters. As we work for ourselves we also think of our contributions to everybody. We are all members of one family, and in working for the union, we are in fact working for ourselves.

(8)

大学的时事学会，明天要开年会了。

去年发生的大事，可多得不得了。年头，有过大国打小国的事。现在大国也好，小国也好，个个都要自主。要是自主不成，不用说，那就得打起来。

年中，又有车子进口的事。在国会开会时，有人说，这事得他做主，又有人说："不是他，是我！"这样说来说去，大家都不开心，后来只好不了了之。

国会在过年的前后开成了。这次国会主要是为了国人出国的事，有人说现在出国，还不是时候；又有人说，大家都得出去看看，看过之后，就会知道要怎么做。

大都会中心的地道工事，开工已经一年，现在进行得怎么样了？工人在什么时候可以进工会？大学几时可以开学？国家几时起用发明家？车子出口的行情为什么不好？现行的国情，有什么不对？…

这么多的事情，都要在明天的会上说明。大家都来想一想，想到什么，就说什么。这样就可以知道，以前有什么不对，还有，以后要怎么进行。

The University Current Affairs Society will convene its annual meeting tomorrow.

The past year had seen numerous major events happening to some countries.

There was a big nation that bullied a small nation at the beginning of the year. But nowadays be it big or small, every nation seeks to be independent. If it fails in its bid to be independent, needless to say, war will break out.

Something else that happened in the middle of the year concerned car importation. The issue was debated in Parliament because certain people wanted to have a say in it.

There was much disagreement which resulted in unhappiness, and in the end the matter remained unresolved.

The last Parliamentary session ended at the end of the year. The main agenda concerned overseas ventures. Some said it was time to venture overseas, others disagreed. Those in favour felt that everyone should go abroad so that they could develop more insight into things.

The underground project beneath the Metropolitan Centre has been underway for one year. What is its progress? When can its workers join the union?

There are many other issues: when will the university commence its new academic term? When will our nation make good use of the services of inventors? Why isn't the car export not so good? Is anything wrong with our present political situation?

There are so many matters to be discussed at the annual meeting tomorrow. Let's all give some thoughts to it and express what we think. In this way we'll be able to know where we have gone wrong in the past as well as how we should go in future.

(9)

　　五年前，老头子还在的时候，一家大小，天明就下地做工，从来没个二心。后来有个好 (hào) 事的人，来对老大说："看得出，你会是个出人头地的人，为什么成天在家里，不出去走动走动，上上学？"

　　老大心里想："可不是？这年头要是没上过学，是不会有人看得起的"。老大走了以后，他老子很不好过，就对老二说："你可不要学他，成天走来走去，人不做工，就没得吃！"

　　老二天天和老头下地，看看又过了一年。有一天，以前那个好事的又来了。他对老二说："不是我说，你这也不成个样，你看你家老大，人家走过大都会，上过学，还成了家，有了家小了！现在做的事可大了！"

　　老二少说也二十大几，老大不小的了，一说老大成了家，就心动了。没和他老子说，大后天天一明就走了。

　　老头一个人在家，现在地里的工也做不下去了。他口里不说，心里不上不下的，可想他们了。老大老二就这么一走了之，从来也没回来看看他老人家。

　　老人后来就这么过去了，这是一年前的事了。

When the old man was still alive five years ago, every member of the family would go to work in the field at daybreak without a second thought. Later a well-intentioned person said to the eldest son, "I can see that you have the ability to be a successful person one day. Why do you keep to your home all day long and not go out to see the world? Why don't you go to school?"

The eldest son thought to himself, "It does make sense; nowadays nobody will respect you if you don't have an education." So he left home, and this upset the old man. He said to his second son, "Don't you follow in his footsteps, and come or leave as you please. If we do not work, we will have nothing to eat."

The second son went to work in the field with his father every day for another year.

One day, the same well-intentioned man came by again. He said to the second son, "I don't really want to say this, but if you carry on in this way you would achieve nothing. Look at your eldest brother, he has been to the big cities, has got an education and has even set up a family. Now he does important things at work."

The second son, who was in his late twenties and not much younger than his older brother, was affected by the fact that his brother had already married. So three days later, he too left home, without informing his father about it.

Left all alone at home, the old man was unable to carry on with the work in the field. Although he did not express it openly, he missed his two sons deeply. They had left home suddenly and, since then, had never returned to pay the old man a visit.

Then one year ago, the old man passed away.